Don't Ever Give Up

Bob Spurlin
2101 Glenwood Drive • Hartselle, AL 35640
256 - 773-0295

A Product Of
Sain Publications
P. O. Box 616 • Pulaski, TN 38478
931-363-6905

Preface

This book was the brainchild of my publisher and good friend, Paul Sain. He mentioned the idea of *"Don't Ever Give Up"* as the title and it would give me a jumping off place to address specific issues in our daily lives. Confronting subject matter like: human suffering, loss of a spouse, loss of a child, facing a bedridden existence, challenge to caregivers, troubled marriages, disorderly children, loneliness, addictions, and so forth. Since normalcy of life changed forever with a crippling disease and being bedridden for nearly nine years, it enables me to write on such subject matter. My hope is that coping with such a disease and the confinement associated with such a bedridden condition would give me special insights into the problems discussed.

Life is uncertain at best and to see changes take place positively and negatively should be no surprise. As the eloquent apostle Paul said,

> This one thing I do, forgetting those things which are behind, and reaching forth to those things which are before. I press toward the mark for the prize of the high calling of God in Christ Jesus (Phil. 3:13-14).

The Mayo Clinic diagnosed my illness as multiple sclerosis in the progressive stage in August of 1995. Four days later our only daughter, Bethany Ann, 16, succumbed to a terminal automobile accident compounding the shocking news already announced. A series of treatments, experimental drugs, physical and occupational therapy, resulting with a week at the HealthSouth Rehabilitation Center in Huntsville, AL provided no improvement.

Massive doses of prednisone and other trial and error methods took place, however positive results did not occur as the decline of the disease continues. Neurologists, neurosurgeons, and countless other medical personnel suggested to us there was no available treatment to correct the problem.

For nearly six months I was able to preach from my wheelchair following the initial diagnosis. According to my audience, those hearing me before and after my disability considered my preaching more attentive to the practical problems of life such as human suffering, and other topics that came before my illness. One of my last appointments before an exacerbation restricted me to my hospital bed, a sister congregation invited me to speak during their morning worship. This appointment provided an opportunity to speak before a large television audience. Addressing the assembly from my wheelchair, my subject, *"A God of the Hills, but not of the Valleys"* examined a serious subject. Many believe God blesses only those during times of plenty and turns a deaf ear when facing times of misery. This, of course, is a total rejection of word and practice on the pages of Holy Writ. It would have been easy for me, or others surrendering to such disastrous events, to abandon God while crying, *"woe is me."* Job, Joseph, Paul, and other Biblical characters did not abandon God when circumstances seemed overwhelming, nor should we.

Since the crippling disease of MS took control of my life there has been a steady decline with exacerbations taking place reducing movement and limited acts. Changes taking place made it compulsory to use a cane, walker, wheelchair, and finally limited to a hospital bed. My wife, Beverly, has been a loving and compassionate caregiver giving attention to my every need. Being a responsible second grade teacher, while keeping a spotless house, plus the scores of other duties that tug at her time speak volumes of her as a caregiver. Those that are thrust into this position do not seek or ask for it, but take it on with devotion and dedication, as their loved one is dependent on their care. Rarely do caregivers get the recognition or credit they deserve, but go about their business giving attention to a spouse or other family member not expecting praise.

Serving as minister in churches of Christ for thirty years has been a satisfying and major focus of my life. However, confinement to a hospital bed is not the vision expected, which preceded my 50th birthday. Brethren Tom Holland and Paul Sain provided great encouragement for me to write a book, which at the time, was an impossible task to imagine. My family subsequently insisted that we buy a computer that would allow me to use the word processor by writing such a book. For a time using the keyboard in the conventional way was satisfactory, but the multiple sclerosis continued to leave my right hand and arm almost unusable. God has given me the ability and technology to write two books, **Tackling Life's Troubles** and **Dial 911: Essentials to Living Life in the 21st Century.**

Unable to write in the traditional way a special program became available for my computer, Dragon Pad voice activated program. No longer able to use my right arm and hand, I speak to the computer, which translates the spoken word into printed material. Book orders began pouring in from individuals as book orders went to forty states and seven foreign nations. This exceeded all expectations with three printings needed. Although my physical health has serious limits, yet the benefits to help those that face distress daily is a blessing never expected. It is with deep gratitude the heavenly Father has provided a medium that allows me to continue teaching through the written word. Remember, long after we have passed from this life will the power of the written word continue to influence those for good. It is our hope that **Don't Ever Give Up** will be helpful and edifying to the reader.

Bob Spurlin
March 2003

Dedication

This book, **Don't Ever Give Up** is dedicated to my family, who has been a source of constant encouragement to me in my writings since my illness began in the spring of 1995. My wife, Beverly, especially has lifted my spirits and continues to make my daily existence bearable while rousing my soul to sing. A special word of thanks is expressed to my son, Paul, and my brothers Jere and Calvin, who have faithfully bathed me each week while performing other duties as needed.

Thanks to all faithful preachers and elders that have faithfully discharged their duty in the proclamation of the gospel and providing leadership for the church of the Lord Jesus Christ. Countless elders and ministers of the gospel have brought awareness to our plight and given help by bringing attention to our two previous books. We trust that such will be the case for this book as well.

Special recognition is expressed to brother Garland Elkins for writing the introduction of the book and the constant encouragement provided by him and his wonderful wife Corinne. My gratitude is expressed to brother Paul Sain for the constancy of his support and publishing my two previous books. Paul has been a dear friend and a constant lifter of my spirits.

-Bob Spurlin-
March 2003

Introduction

His body was twisted and distorted, but his attitude was so radiant. When asked *"with such disability, so difficult to get around, so deprived of so many things of life, how is it that you are still so radiant?"* He quickly responded *"my disease never reached my heart!"* The above describes, to some degree, brother Bob Spurlin. He has suffered long and much, yet has borne his problems valiantly. His courage and endurance would put many of us to shame. When Paul learned his *"thorn in the flesh"* would continue, he was willing to bear whatever was necessary under the circumstances, for the Lord and His work:

> And he hath said unto me, My grace is sufficient for thee: for my power is made perfect in weakness. Most gladly therefore will I rather glory in my weakness, that the power of Christ may rest upon me (2 Cor. 12:9).

> Take, brethren, for an example of suffering and of patience, the prophets who spoke in the name of the Lord. Behold, we call them blessed that endured. Ye have heard of the patience of Job, and have seen the end of the Lord, how that the Lord is full of pity and merciful (James 5:10,11).

When I think of Bob and his suffering, I think of noble Job and the prophets.

Another class comes to mind also, the wonderful, devoted, and dedicated gospel preachers, who laid the foundation for us to build upon; their struggles, long periods away from their families, scarcely paid enough to survive and lacking in convenient ways to travel. We know good health, and prosperity are not a prerequisite for going to heaven. I am very thankful that brother Spurlin dedicated his life to being a gospel preacher and he chose a marvelous companion to help him succeed. They have made a great team. I am thankful also that God let our paths cross. For thirty years he has preached the gospel and even now handicapped, continues to give of his very best so that others can be blessed. His writings have rendered a valuable service and so many of us cannot relate to his experiences, though sad and regretted they are, have given others courage to keep keeping on. A great admirer once said of brother N.B. Hardeman, *"Brother Hardeman is a great preacher and does not know it."* That can easily be said of brother Spurlin. His character and reputation are sterling.

When I think of the worthy woman of Proverbs 31 Bob's lovely wife Beverly comes to mind.

> Who can find a virtuous woman? For her price is far above rubies. The heart of her husband doeth safely trust in her, so that he shall have no need of spoil. She will do him good and not evil all the days of her life (Prov. 31:10-12).

Beverly is industrious, keeping their house and yard to perfection, while teaching to supplement their mounting medical expenses. She does not eat her bread with idleness. She has climbed her mountain with grace, love and courage. My wife and I are blessed to know this godly couple. Their E-mails and newsletters have been inspiring to us. If they have a *"down time"* they do not communicate that to others. They hold a special place in our hearts.

Bob Spurlin's three books reflect his conviction, dedication and faithfulness to the Lord and His church. His first book is entitled **Tackling Life's Troubles**. Believe me he is an authority on this subject. His second is: **Dial 911: Essentials to Living** and this volume is **Don't Ever Give Up**. This is so appropriate for these two exemplary Christians, who have weathered the storms, while most of us have endured only the showers of life. Calvin Coolidge ·

said "*His wife had borne his infirmities for 25 years and had done so, gracefully.*" This can be said of Beverly. She is to be admired for standing by her husband in a difficult and crucial time. "*Love in your heart is not there to stay, love in your heart is there to give away.*" Paul wrote "*and let us not be weary in well doing: for in due season we shall reap, if we faint not*" (Gal. 6:9).

It is my hope and prayer that this book will be given wide and favorable distribution. If given wide circulation two things will follow: First, great good will be accomplished. Second, the profit from this book will help to defray brother Spurlin's tremendous medical expenses.

Garland Elkins
March 27, 2003

Table Of Contents

1. Don't Ever Give-Up 15

2. Don't Ever Give Up —
   Biblical Formula For Facing Life 27

3. Don't Ever Give Up —
   When It Comes To Human Suffering 37

4. Don't Ever Give Up —
   When Faced With The Loss Of A Spouse 51

5. Don't Ever Give Up —
   When Faced With The Loss Of A Child 63

6. Don't Ever Give Up —
   When Faced With A Bedridden Condition 73

7. Don't Ever Give Up —
   A Challenge To Caregivers 85

8. Don't Ever Give Up —
   A State Of Loneliness 97

9. Don't Ever Give Up —
   When Parents Face Disorderly Children 111

10. Don't Ever Give Up —
    The Modern Family in Trouble 125

11. Don't Ever Give Up —
    When Faced With Financial Problems 137

12. Don't Ever Give Up—
      When Faced With Addictions 151

13. Don't Ever Give Up—
      Testing Our Faith 173

14. Don't Ever Give Up—
      Suicide: A Christian Viewpoint 183

15. Don't Ever Give Up—
      Shocking Events Do Happen 223

16. Don't Ever Give Up—
      Our Health, A Blessing From God 239

Chapter One

Don't Ever Give Up!

The difficulties and trials of life can be overwhelming at times. Regardless of our station in life; whether we be rich, poor, high on the social ladder or social outcast, misfortune and hardship will occur to each of us. Jesus is the great physician and knowing his patient, man, He is able to provide the prescription enabling us to cope with the difficulties of life (Luke 5:31-32). "Don't Ever Give-Up" is not just a pleasant slogan to the ear, but rather it is the only formula allowing us to meet the hurts and hardships that confront us.

Paul continually warned the Galatian Christians not to become "weary in well doing for in due season we shall reap, if we faint not...I desire that ye faint not" (Rom. 2:7; Gal. 6:9; 2 Thess. 3:13). Summarizing, Paul is stating in effect "Don't Ever Give-Up," as a substitute to the tragic circumstances that come to pass.

During our human experience, no doubt, we have

all engaged in discussions of unfortunate crises by stating "why me" or "why did this happen?" Life can be difficult to understand with hardships, terminal disease, unexpected death, and other suffering. These are difficulties that occur among the human family periodically and decide our character and spiritual well-being. From a personal perspective enjoying a full and rich life with a wonderful wife, two children and the sheer pleasure of working with the church of the Lord were the crowning happiness for me. Our family life exceeded all expectations of joy and happiness, thus the negative forces of evil could not be expected. It is a false delusion to think we will not confront the horrific episodes that Satan will bring on us. "Don't Ever Give Up" is the only formula to follow despite the unbelievable heartache that can be thrust on us.

A PERSONAL ILLUSTRATION

The author of these lines became ill in 1995 with progressive multiple sclerosis that has caused a bedridden existence for almost eight years. Losing one's dignity and being dependent on your spouse and other family members for the most basic care became a humbling experience. Never was it ever imagined that a preacher enthusiastic about his work with an all-consuming schedule expected his work shortened to the life of a shut-in. A fundamental lesson learned by this author is coming to grips with the unexpected. This physical condition, coupled with a useless and fatal automobile accident to our daughter, seemed impossible to bear. My wife and I faced shock and delirium, which defied human description. Such misery was not because our daughter faced an eternal world unprepared to meet the judge of all men. Conversely, it was because of human reason that separated us from our daughter and the vacuum created in the family. "Don't Ever Give Up" was the only approach as the broken heart was dependent on God to recover.

As a minister of the gospel for three decades, many horrible and ghastly events has come to my attention. Counseling Christians and non-Christians alike resolves seemingly impossible difficulties and trials. At first many would place culpability on others, while most will seek to cast all blame on our God. The supreme God of the universe is not the author of destruction and calamity. Paul, the apostle, writes, "God is not the author of confusion, but of peace" (1 Cor. 14:33). James writes, "let no man say when he is tempted, I am tempted of God; for God cannot be tempted with the evil, neither tempteth he any man" (James 1:13). God does not cause one to sin; neither does he cause disaster or calamity. Our eternal God has all in control even though, at times it seems the world has gone awry. God, the creator of heaven and earth were according to the divine pattern, put the sun and moon in motion with all other galaxies in their place. On the fourth day God made the greater light to rule the day and the lesser light to rule the night (Gen. 1:14-19). Many have tried to place blame on God and so He becomes an easy target. When something evil or unknown happens that we cannot control, instead of accepting responsibility we find it easy to place blame on someone else, or on God himself.

The book of Job reveals the "sons of God coming to present themselves to the Lord and Satan also accompanied them" (Job 1:6). The Lord quizzed Satan "Hast thou considered my servant Job, that there is none like him in the earth, a perfect and upright man, one that feared God and escheweth (shuns) the evil?" (Job 1:8). "Does Job fear God for naught (nothing)?" (Job 1:9). Satan raises a question, which charges God to explain why Job has been a faithful servant. Satan is the cause that seeks to ensnare the souls of men to sin. Our enemy sets forth the proposition to God that Job's faithfulness to the Lord emanates from the material possessions given to him. Satan, the source of all evil, charged God that he had set a hedge, or kept him away from all evil, blessed the work of his hands, and his substance (cattle) increased in the land (Job 1:9-10). Satan sets forth a proposition that if God will put His hand on Job and touch all he has then the faithful servant, Job, will curse the Lord to the face. Satan's thesis about God's beloved servant, Job, was that his devotion and faithfulness was dependent on God blessing him. The Lord gave Satan the power to do anything he wanted with Job, however he could not put forth his hand to destroy or take the life of the faithful servant of God.

Satan used the power to do all the evil against Job save taking his life. A servant reported that all sons and daughters of Job suffered death when a great wind fell on them. The Sabeans took the oxen and asses while killing the servants of their master Job. Another servant told Job the sheep and servants died in a fire and only the one servant told of such a horrible calamity. The Chaldeans formed three bands or raiding parties and swept down on your camels and carried them off and destroyed them with the sword. Then Job rent his mantle (robe), shaved his head and fell down on the ground to worship God. Following all the suffering that came into the life of Job he sinned not and refused to charged God foolishly (Job 1:12-22).

ABE LINCOLN
A BIOGRAPHY IN FAILURE

1. Difficult childhood
2. Less than one year formal schooling
3. Failed in business in 1831
4. Defeated for legislature, 1832
5. Again failed in business, 1833
6. Elected to legislature, 1834
7. Fiancee died, 1835
8. Defeated for Speaker, 1838
9. Defeated for Elector, 1840
10. Married, wife a burden, 1842
11. Only one of his four sons lived past 18
12. Defeated for Congress, 1843
13. Elected to Congress, 1846
14. Defeated for Congress, 1848
15. Defeated for Senate, 1855

16. Defeated for Vice-President, 1856
17. Defeated for Senate, 1858
18. Elected President, 1860

Accepting failure in the positive sense becomes effective when you believe that the right to fail is as important as the right to succeed. Abraham Lincoln, 16th President of the United States, did not allow failure to paralyze him from being a success. One of the greatest statesman and politicians in our nation's history could have used any number of excuses for not trying again. Despite all the adversity he endured, Abe Lincoln would not be deprived of the success he longed for. Many noted inventors and entrepreneurs have failed before reaching the pinnacle of success. Henry Ford forgot to put reverse gear in his first automobile and Thomas Edison lost two million dollars on an invention to be of little or no value. We learn from the example of these men that giving up was not in their character, but perseverance and enduring till the end were.

It is impossible to succeed without suffering. If you are successful and have not suffered, someone has suffered for you and if you are suffering without succeeding, perhaps someone may succeed after you. But there is not success without suffering. Like many of us that have ill health, we seldom value the importance of health untill it is lost.

INGREDIENTS THAT AID
THOSE TO NEVER GIVE-UP

1. A friend with whom you can talk to daily
2. Someone that cares about you and will provide encouragement

3. Talk to a person that will be honest and truthful in giving counsel
4. Get guidance from those that have persevered great hardship
5. Read and study Romans 8:31-39

JOB'S EXAMPLE–NEVER GIVING UP

If all the suffering and hardship Job endured was not enough, Satan charged the Lord that his servant would curse him to the face if his flesh were smitten. The Lord said to Satan, "Behold, he is in thine hand; but save his life" (Job 2:6). The body of this faithful man of God covered was with sore boils from the sole of his foot to his crown (head). The pain was so terrible that "he sat down among the ashes" (Job 2:8). For the first time Job's wife speaks saying, "dost thou still retain thine own integrity? Curse God, and die" (Job 2: 9). Job's strength was in God and regardless of what his wife said, his loyalty to God was steadfast despite his wife's wishes. Job was not one to "ask why," but answered his wife "thou speakest as one of the foolish women speaketh. What? Shall we receive good at the hand of God, and shall we not receive evil? In all this did not Job sin with his lips" (Job 2:10). If we receive the good and positive blessings, may we question God and ask why, when evil visits our door? Job's spiritual state, embedded to the rock of ages, would not fall to Satan and his vices. Job's wife, friends, loss of property, livestock nor the loss of all his children would not shake the faith of this patriarch of the Old Testament. When calamity and heartache strikes at our door may we draw strength from our faith in God, as did Job. When alone and life seems its worst, "Don't Ever Give-Up" is the only sane and sensible approach in confronting the trials of life (James 4:14-17).

Sir Winston Churchill was one of the most distinguished world leaders, politician,.and steadying voices during World War II. During Great Britain's darkest hour when their nation was under attack by Hitler's war machine, the Prime Minister of England was crying out that they would never surrender to the tyrant of Germany. Churchill mobilized his country as well as ours to stamp out the evil of Nazism. Following the success of World War II, the headmaster of Harrow Preparatory School invited Churchill to speak at an assembly of all students. The student body learned the Prime Minister was an alumnus of the school, and that everyone should be attentive and take notes. After a lengthy and flowery introduction the former student at Harrow Preparatory rose to his feet and said, "Never, never, never give up," after which he sat down. The principal was surprised at such a brief and terse speech, yet what better way to make such a permanent mark on the student body? This was a powerful and practical outlook on life that would shape the approach of how people would conduct their lives.

TOPICS FOR DISCUSSION

1. Why is "Don't Ever Give Up" the solution to the trials of life?

2. How would you reject the common argument, "God is to blame for my misfortune?"

3. Is it accurate to say Abraham Lincoln was a failure? Could you overcome such adversity and rise from the proverbial ashes?

4. Is Winston Churchill's words "Never, never, never give up" a practical approach to live by, or is it too simplistic?

Chapter Two

Biblical Formula For Living Life

S eeking the favor of God, men and women diligently search for the formula of living life. True happiness can only come when Christ is the center of our existence along with serving our fellowman. Far too many have given over to a "love of money that is the root of all evil..." (1 Tim. 6:10). Some mistakenly substitute a life filled with what money can buy rather than the solace gained through living for Christ (Matt. 6:33). Early in my work as a gospel preacher a brother in the congregation, materially blessed, seemed content with his life. He was a man with charisma and personality and had the Midas touch with business and other interests as well. His attendance was consistent and he would lead a song at the monthly singing. Sometime later we learned that this brother during some of his business trips became unfaithful to his wife. This talented man became distracted when he allowed sin to enter his heart. Throughout life we face challenges as choices bring us to our destiny. Moses faced a decision, "choosing rather to suffer affliction with the people of God than to enjoy the pleasures of sin for a season" (Heb. 11:24-25).

Moses gave serious thought to his decision. He considered the effects of the riches and glory of Egypt with the prospect of spending the balance of his days with the people of God. He deliberately chose to travel the course of righteousness rather than to continue in sin. This decision would change the course of human history and fulfill his responsibility to God. Moses saw that to continue in the ease of sin would offer no lasting satisfaction while the choice to serve God would bring complete contentment. We must all come to grips with decisions that will bring our lives closer to our God.

The life we live is the most valued treasure we have. It is with certainty the state of man is difficult at best. Yet, the child of God faces the challenge of evil cares, amusements, and pleasures of the world that would war against our soul (1 Peter 2:11). God's formula for living life offers a road map designed by the Creator (Gen. 1:1, John 1:1-3). The Christian lives before God, which is the beginning of life and so it is here "that (we) might have life, and that we might have it more abundantly" (John 10: 10). The "more abundant" life, suggests eternal life, or spiritual blessings much greater than ever communicated to staff. Jesus came that we may have spiritual blessings and the hope of everlasting life (John 3:16, 36). God's formula for life does not accept the riches of this world as the thesis of living life (Matt. 16:26). Living a full and rich life consists of living by the teachings and rules of almighty God. The increase of material wealth, gaining worldly wisdom, or other carnal appetites will not satisfy our life either in this world or the world that is yet to come.

JAMES STRESSES
THE BREVITY OF LIFE

The inspired writer, James, writes, "Whereas ye know not what shall be on the morrow. What is your life? It is a vapor, that appeared for a little while, and then vanisheth away" (James 4:14). Facing life's troubles compounded with the doubt and confusion that comes with getting a grip on the meaning of life is a great challenge. Countless individuals, troubled with financial difficulties, family problems, and the grasp of happiness itself compel us to ask, "what is the Biblical formula for life."

1. **Life is uncertain at best**–James rejects the common notion that life is certain and man can do as he pleases without consequences. James stressed that we do not have the guarantee of tomorrow. "Whereas ye know not what shall be on the morrow." Those reading the words of James were in denial as it recounts the events that may or may not occur; whether they would live or die; if blessed materially, or stricken with misery. This statement from James is undeniably true, but it is remarkable how often men and women act as if it is false. Life has its limits as

the veil of the future denies us the ability to control what will take place in a single day or hour. Many make their plans as if all will come to pass despite the doubt of what may or may not happen tomorrow. Man does not have a crystal ball and should not make plans, therefore because of the possibility that his life could end at anytime. So, preparation for life mandates that we grab every moment and use it to glorify God (Col. 3:23, Matt. 6:25).

2. **Life is a vapor**–In the original the margin reads, "For it is." The previous question had turned the attention to life as something peculiarly frail, and no calculation could support its permanence. This expression, "It is a vapor," gives a reason for that, because it is a mere vapor. The word "vapor" means a mist, a smoke or such a vapor as we see coming from a stream of water. In addition that which lies on the mountainside on the morning, or as floats for a little time in the air, but which declines by the rising sun, leaving not a trace behind. The comparison of life with a vapor is common, and is as beautiful as it is just.

3. **For that ye ought to say**–James stated that his readers were boastfully saying, "We will go into the city, remain a year and buy and sell, and get gain" (James 4:13). James states in the practical terms of life that we should admit our dependence on God, and have the judgment that life and success are subject to His will. James states, clearly, what "we" intend to do

is offensive when God holds the key to life. True happiness comes when we give full submission in obedience to God.

4. **If the Lord will we shall live**–This is proper, because we are dependent on Him for life, and equally dependent on Him for success. God alone can keep us, and He only can bless the fruit of our hands. In a thousand ways He can spoil our efforts, for all are under His control. We need not travel far in life to see how all that we have is in the hands of God, or to learn how easily He can frustrate us if He pleases. We cannot state that our meager success will come by our efforts alone; any individual honor, success, or victories in life can only come through our dependence on God.

Paul, the apostle, writing to the Christians at Philippi wrote on the general theme of Christian joy. It might surprise you to know the apostle completed this letter while in prison. The attitude of Paul is honest and joyful when he faced the circumstances of his life in prison. "But I would ye should understand, that the things which happened to me have fallen out rather to the furtherance of the gospel" (Phil. 1:12). This prisoner of Christ considered his bonds (imprisonment) a circumstance that allowed him to preach the gospel as it echoed throughout the palace and in other places (Phil. 1:13-14). Often we allow negative conditions to cloud our thinking, thus preventing many from making an optimistic contribution. Instead of Paul remaining on the dark side, the bonds he was enduring, he spoke of his brothers and sisters as "My joy and crown, so stand fast in the Lord, my dearly beloved" (Phil. 4:1).

LET US CONSIDER GOD'S FORMULA FOR LIVING LIFE (Phil. 3:13-14)

1. **Forget those things which are behind**–In the previous statement Paul states, "This one thing I do." Thus, Paul had one aim, one purpose, and one objective to achieve. The singleness of purpose and rare success enjoyed is dependent on our ability to overcome the distractions that blind us. Forgetting those items that are behind will cause one to go back as the example of Lot's wife confirms (Luke 9:62, 17:32). If our attention becomes cloudy for one moment it could easily mean the loss of our crown. Similarly, a failure to use rows or paddles to steer the boat will cause us to drift off course. Some have suggested that Paul is alluding to the Greek races. One running the race would not look behind, as it would take your eye off the goal or finish line.

2. **Reaching forth to those things which are before**–"Reaching forth" comes from the Greek word *epekteino*, which is in the middle voice meaning "to stretch forward as one would reach for a more desirable piece of fruit" (Vine's Dictionary). Obviously the apostle is using the Greek games as a metaphor to suggest the picture of the athlete reaching, and

stretching with every fiber of his being to lunge across the finish line. The winner of the contest became victorious as the judge gave a crown or garland that anointed the winner's head. Faithful Christians will learn the true meaning of life when reaching for the crown of glory, which is freedom from the stench of sin. Repeatedly the words from Holy Writ reminds us, "Therefore leaving the doctrine of the first principles of Christ, let us go on to perfection" (Heb. 6:1). Reaching forward is the key bringing us to a fulfilling life and a failure to do so will cause the child of God to come short of the expectations of our eternal God.

3. **Press toward the mark for the prize**–"Mark" comes from the Greek kata meaning goal or bear down. To press toward the mark is the goal that Christians must have in finding the prize. Winning the prize comes from aiming at the target, also as the archer has his eye fixed on the mark and releases the arrow from the bow. The prize of the Christian is the crown that is incorruptible in heaven. The more fit we grow for heaven the faster we must press towards it. The mark we aspire for is heaven, because it is that which every devoted Christian has in his eye. Paul was a prolific example in following this formula with a single-minded purpose. The apostles' inspired words encourage us, "Set your affection on things above, not on things on the earth" (Col. 3:2). This biblical formula will work if disciples of Christ will incorporate it into their daily life.

TOPICS FOR DISCUSSION

1. What is the one item discussed in the lesson that will hinder living a full life? Why is it at the root of our problems?

2. If life is a vapor, why do so many fail to comprehend it's meaning?

3. Explain Paul's three-point formula of living a fruitful life (Phil. 3:13-15)?

Chapter Three

When It Comes To Human Suffering

There is not a single person who has not endured human suffering. It seems that some people go through more than their share of suffering, but such is the normalcy of life. Many of us have witnessed someone cry out, "Why me, God!" Because of inadequate answers to their cry, human suffering wrecked their faith. These are real people needing real answers to real problems!

God does not exempt us from the problems of human suffering simply because we are His children. How ironic to hear Christians express the opinion that we should be immune to pain or suffering. God does promise us a way to endure and bear-up under the troubles that drive us to the edge. The world does not understand the meaning or the purpose of life. The world thinks the philosophy of hedonism is the answer to life. Webster defines hedonism, "The doctrine that pleasure or happiness is the sole or chief good in life." Too often we hear those of the world live by

"Whatever makes me happy" or "whatever makes the majority happy" as the single pursuit of humanity. Life's meaning, according to the world, is that which brings human suffering. The Bible, the inspired word of God, teaches the meaning of life. God said, "Let us hear the conclusion of the whole matter: Fear God, and keep his commandments: for this it the whole duty of man" (Eccl. 12:13). The Bible affirms certain fundamentals that will answer the question of human suffering and pain.

"WHY, LORD" IS THE QUESTION

There is a question that is as old as creation, and as recent as the latest newscast: "Why? Why does God allow suffering, sorrow, heartache, and death, even among His own children?" This question asked by Job, has come from every curious person who has walked on the face of the earth, and who believes in God. This question was asked by a Christian, who lost two sons in an automobile accident, his wife died of cancer, and his youngest son died of a drug overdose. Knowing the family allowed me to discuss with the surviving family member the horrific series of events. This husband and father, with extended family members, could only say, "Why, God?" The author and his family, like so many others, have faced disaster with the loss of our 16-year-old daughter, who died prematurely in an automobile accident. Four days later doctors discovered multiple sclerosis in my body and shortly later a bedridden existence began. The strongest of Christians will have serious questions .

stirred within him demanding answers when our faith becomes stretched to the limit.

Is human suffering the work of God Himself? Is it the work of Satan? Or is it simply the natural results in a world of cause and effect. God has created a world governed by natural laws: (1) Laws of cause and effect; (2) Laws of action and reaction; (3) Laws of sowing and reaping. If we violate these laws, the cost is often disastrous. Stepping off a twenty-five-story building will surely cause the loss of life because of the "Law of Gravity." Blaming others and even God is a pointless exercise when an unintentional act occurs. Daily we read in the newspaper about those running in front of an automobile or driving carelessly, which causes heartbreak beyond imagination. Is blaming God proper when one becomes obsessed to alcohol, tobacco, illegal drugs and other foreign substances that shortens the lifespan of individuals? Many have suffered untimely death when susceptible to contagious diseases and other life threatening illness. Human suffering does not happen because we are evil or good. Much of the suffering experienced in life is the result of violating natural laws. We should not, however, dispel the role that Satan plays in the human suffering that plagues man. The example of Job is a clear example of Satan's evil deeds.

The answer comes from the Word of God where such encouragement is the result of our dependence on the Divine pattern. Paul stressed that God's Word will comfort us during our darkest hour, for "We have such a hope" (2 Cor. 3:12). Overcoming the loss of a loved one, enduring terminal illness, and other difficulties by human suffering can be a threat to our faith. Paul underlined the value of the inspired word as he declared: "Now, I commend you to God, and the word of his grace, which will build you up, and to give you an inheritance among all them which are sanctified" (Acts 20:32).

BLESSINGS FROM HUMAN SUFFERING

1. **Suffering prevents us from falling in love with the world.** The world can be so appealing and attractive that our heads can easily veer away from that heavenly home. John writes, "Love not the world, neither the things that are in the world. If any man love the world, the love of the Father is not in him" (1 John 2:15). The enemy of humanity, Satan, has an arsenal full of weapons to seduce our souls. Using the glamour and appeal of the world is a primary tool and he uses it with great success. Paul states plainly, "...For we are not ignorant of his (Satan) devices" (2 Cor. 2:11).

My friends, we are not of this world. In fact, we are simple "pilgrims" passing through a land that is not our own (1 Peter 2:11). God has prepared a place for us, which should inspire others to reach that home in glory (John 14:1-3). This heavenly city should be the wish of every believer to go there and reject the world from getting in our eye. Demas, Ananias and Sapphira, and Simon the sorcerer, among others became enticed and baited by a love of the world (2 Tim. 4:10; Acts 5:1-10; Acts 8:16-19). Let us not repeat the mistakes of those characters of the past, but learn from faithful servants like Abraham. "For he looked for a city which hath foundations, whose builder and maker is God" (Heb 11:10).

If there were no suffering in our lives then what would compel us to leave the world? Enraptured with the present world will nullify the wish for the "eternal" home, and so our preparation for it. If we were lacking of human suffering then why should we consider the mansions prepared for us? When human suffering knocks at our door we either rely on God for comfort or on the emptiness of the world. Suffering in all its forms will cause us to lose an attraction for the world because God and only God can supply that which we need (Heb. 11:1-3).

2. **Suffering has the potential of bringing out the best in us.** Many individuals or families that have faced human suffering in its various forms either by death of a love one, or facing a disabling or terminal disease have found that it will present a real test to us. Conversely, those viewing human disaster have the opportunity to serve in various ways. As a preacher of the gospel seeing those who endure horrific circumstances in various ways has given opportunities to relieve those in different ways. Many have responded to those suffering souls by offering support. Paul counsels the Galatians: "Bear ye one another's burdens, and so fulfill the law of Christ" (Gal. 6: 2). It is a breathe of fresh air to see Christians extend encouragement to those in pain.

During times of disaster, what better way to show our concern than by holding a hand, preparing a meal, or helping one that needs financial support with a contribution when needed? Those who have faced great loss, or prolonged financial ruin would find it useful to receive a donation. One cannot imagine the help it would mean to receive the tender kindness of those extending a hand of compassion. Remember the stirring words of Jesus: "For I was a hungred, and ye gave me meat (food): I was thirsty, and ye gave me drink: I was a stranger, and ye took me in: Naked, and ye clothed me: I was sick, and ye visited me" (Matt. 25:35-36). Perhaps one reason the early Christians rejoiced in their trials is because they understood that misfortunes and suffering would develop character (Rom. 5:3-4).

3. **Suffering, like fire removing impurities from a stone, also purifies us.** Peter stresses suffering can be like fire purifying gold. He writes: "The trial of your faith, being much more precious than of gold that perisheth, though it be tried with fire..." (1 Peter 1:6-7). All of us will face difficulties and trials, which will put our faith to the test. How we respond to the troubles in life will decide the character we have. The inspired writer, James, writes, "Count it all joy when you fall into divers temptations (trials). Knowing this, the trying of your faith worketh patience" (James 1:2-3). It is only when our faith passes the test that patience can grow. Abraham accepted the test that would bring him to the sacrificial altar where his son,

Isaac, came before God as a lamb (Gen. 22:1-12). This author has often prayed for patience. It was after the loss of our precious daughter, coupled with the diagnosis of multiple sclerosis reducing me to a bedridden existence, that patience became realized.

4. Suffering will lead us to our dependence on God. Men and women find it difficult to be submissive to God. There is a natural resistance for man to give-in to Satan with all the temptations he places in our path. The "lust of the flesh," the "lust of the eyes," and "pride of life" are the three avenues by which Satan seduces man to sin (1 John 2:16). With this as a backdrop in man's thinking, it is little wonder that he feels self-sufficient thinking that God is unimportant. A talented young man in full compliance to the old law (Law of Moses) asked Jesus what he needed to do to secure eternal life. Jesus, learning of the young man's devotion to the Law of Moses, responded to the question posed to Him. Jesus aware of the young man's traits, said: "Go and sell that thou hast, and give to the poor, and thou shalt have treasure in heaven" (Matt. 19:21). The young man hearing this "went away sorrowful: for he had great possessions" (Matt. 19:22).

Conversely, human suffering is the common denominator for all, making us equally dependent on God. Having doctor after doctor tell me that treatment was unavailable to relieve me of a crippling disease makes me feel more dependent on God. Let us all realize that we are one breath away from death making us dependent on our Creator. We will not get to death's door before realizing our need for God. As Paul announced to the Athenians: "In Him we live and move and have our being" (Acts 17:28).

5. **Suffering souls produce sympathetic hearts.** The words "strength," "steadfastness," and "love" connect with the term sympathy. Sympathy is not only a matter of duty; it is also a matter of generosity. Those suffering people seek the care and concern from individuals willing to reach out and serve those hurting. A sympathetic heart is one of the central characteristics of the child of God. Paul stressed to the Corinthians the value of affliction. Paul writes: "The God of all comfort, who comforted us in all tribulation, that we may be able to comfort them which are in any trouble, by the comfort wherewith we ourselves are comforted of God" (2 Cor. 1:3-4).

Compassionate and sympathetic hearts will readily comfort others in their affliction. It was the Savior that told the Parable of Good Samaritan, which contrasted the priest and Levite, insensitive to the man left for dead, with the Samaritan who raptly attended to the needy man. The Samaritan, "When he saw him (victim), had compassion on him and bound up his wounds, pouring in oil and wine, set him on his own beast, and brought him to the inn, and took care of him" (Luke 10:33-34). Human suffering did not move the pious religious leaders referred to in this parable, yet the good Samaritan moved with compassion when he saw the pitiful man left for dead. Some have difficulty showing sympathy without seeing the person enduring great pain and anguish. To experience suffering will make us more likely to "weep with those who weep" (Rom. 12:15). Let us all produce sympathetic hearts to reach out and serve those suffering souls. Jesus said: "It is more blessed to give than to receive" (Acts 20:35). This is a fundamental teaching that will make us all better Christians.

6. **Suffering will enrich our prayer life.** As a gospel preacher for thirty years many important truths became stressed in the classroom and pulpit. Public and private prayer has been a priority in my teaching and preaching. While working with congregations my objective was to practice Paul's admonition: "Pray without ceasing" (1 Thess. 5:17). However, following the death of our daughter, 16, a totally confined and a bedridden existence caused by multiple sclerosis a normal life style was thwarted. This crippling disease moved my prayer life to a level never before realized. Family and Christian friends have often quizzed, "How do you cope with such a confining existence?" To say that MS has not been exasperating and frustrating over the last eight years would reduce the seriousness of the disease. My prayer life has subsequently reached a loftiness not previously known. Perhaps the total confinement with serious reflection and meditation on my physical condition has caused me to realize the seriousness of prayer. My wife and family is attendant to all my physical needs; however, dependency on God to aid me

physically and spiritually is essential of the heavenly Father.

My prayer life began early in life and after becoming a Christian, its importance increased dramatically. Fervent and wholehearted prayer becomes a daily practice with a deep sense of reverence and reliance on God. We have the assurance the prayers of Christians have gone to the heavenly throne of grace, and conversely my prayers go up daily for countless people asking for such. Perseverance and persistence during the endless days of confinement, caused by this disease, has heightened my prayer life with a keen sense of devotion to our Creator.

David put his pen in the inkwell of inspiration and wrote the following: "Give ear to my words, O Lord, consider my meditation. Hearken to the voice of my cry, my King, and my God: for to thee will I pray. My voice shalt thou hear in the morning, O Lord; in the morning will I direct my prayer to thee, and will look up" (Psalm 5:1-3).

CONCLUSION

Because of the hope and grandeur of heaven, human suffering is but a twinkling of a moment. Heaven would not have the appeal it does if it were not for the illnesses of this life. When describing heaven, John said, "God will wipe away every tear from their eyes; there shall be no more death, nor sorrow, nor crying; and there shall be no more pain, for the former things have passed away" (Rev. 21:4). Let us now note the "former things" as those critical items of this world, such as death, sorrow, and pain. In heaven there is life, light, and liberty from sin, pain, and death.

TOPICS FOR DISCUSSION

1. Why does the world have difficulty in understanding human suffering?

2. What philosophy discussed in this lesson affects so many today?

3. What are some blessings that come from human suffering?

4. Name some positive works that we can do to help those that are suffering?

5. How important is a rich prayer life when it comes to from human suffering?

6. What are the natural laws that contribute to human suffering?

Chapter Four
When Faced With The Loss Of A Spouse

As a preacher of the gospel the most difficult duty faced is providing comfort and support to those suffering the loss of a loved one. Expressing sympathy to an individual enduring such pain in their loss is a natural extension of our sympathy to the person. There are different levels or degrees in the emptiness and anguish the survivor feels when death takes a loved one. Not everyone will feel the same when death snatches a family member, mother, father, child, or spouse from our lives. Human beings have a different capacity to love, rejoice, and grieve. This writer has suffered the loss of a parent, grandparents, a sibling, and the loss of a child. Never having experienced the loss of a spouse has caused me to enlist the help from a dear sister in Christ who has suffered such a loss. Much of the material below comes from and arranged by sister Avis C. Porter, surviving wife of her deceased husband. Sister Porter's husband, Preston, was a faithful gospel preacher for

40 years. It is with great appreciation that this sister has agreed to share her thoughts on this important subject.

STEPS TO GRIEF RECOVERY

Shock And Disbelief–When the news of your mate's death comes, at first you can hardly believe it has happened! You have just experienced another natural phase of your life. Unless an accident occurs leaving both husband and wife deceased, one spouse will pass before the other in death. Either a sudden or unexpected death, or a prolonged illness followed by the spouse expiring, the result will be the same–shock and disbelief. Human beings are social individuals and the attachment made between husband and wife is one of the closest connections known to the human family. In fact, the apostle Paul used the husband-wife union to show the bond between Christ and the church (Eph. 5:21-33). Coming from such a loss will need weeks or some indefinite period of time, different with each individual. Coming to grips with such an emotional shock is stressful. It will take time to register as the surviving spouse is in some intermediate state striving to get in touch with reality.

Anger–Perhaps you might feel anger that your mate has left you. You may try to convince yourself that it did not happen. You may wonder, "What will I do?" Or, "How will I survive alone?" But, with the Lord's help, you will make it and the adjustment will come in time. Paul writes, "I can do all things through

Christ which strengthenth me" (Phil. 4:13). Look to your inner reservoir of might trusting in the Lord and you will discover strength you did not know was there (Prov. 3:5). It is a shock to realize one is a widow or widower, no longer a part of a couple, but alone. It would profit all of us to talk to others, especially those who have suffered a similar loss. Such conversations will be helpful during the grieving period. The loss of a spouse is an individual matter and thus we suffer at different levels of hurt and pain; however we must all go through the stages of grief. Do not consider it a weakness or failing to cry, men included. Surviving husbands often feel their strength questioned if they show an outburst of emotion, but such is normal and releasing. God has made us with this release for hurting people aiding us in the adjustment period. Remember, "Jesus wept" with Mary and Martha after their brother Lazarus died (John 11:35). Our loved ones and friends may also shed tears because they love you, and your deceased spouse as they feel the agony of our pain. Paul urged Christians' to "rejoice with them that rejoice and weep with them that weep" (Rom. 12:15).

SYMPTOMS OF LOSING A SPOUSE

Loneliness–Regardless of how long your marriage lasted before it's separation at death, when you remain behind, a part of you is gone. No longer are you a couple as changes will occur and adjustments must be made, and the same will be true with your friends who remain a couple. Normalcy as you know it is over and you are no longer considered a couple, which causes a sense of stress with your married friends. If our spouse dies after the children have left home you discover how empty the house is and what a lonely place the house has become. You sleep alone, instead of next to a warm body. You eat your meals on your own and eating out is difficult, if not impossible. There is a great void in being alone, but loneliness comes only in the sense that our spouse is no longer present. The Lord lives with me and I have a Christian home! However, let us always be aware of the Lord's presence. Jesus commissioned his disciples, "Go you therefore, and teach all nations, baptizing them in the name of the Father, and out of the Son, and of the Holy Spirit...And lo I am with you alway, even onto the end of the world" (Matt. 28:19-20). How comforting to know that we will never be alone with Jesus' presence always nearby. The Bible comes with comforting words like "The God of peace be with you all...The God of the Lord Jesus Christ be with you. Amen" (Rom. 15: 33, 16: 20, 24). Loneliness may consume us, however it is not because God and His Word are not available to provide comfort.

Difficulties–If you have not experienced handling finances, taking care of or servicing a car, handling a lawn mower, cooking a meal, making use of the washer and vacuum cleaner may take an adjustment. Many of these duties may be difficult to handle in the beginning, but in time those household tasks will become mastered. This can be an.

opportunity for personal growth and development. When you do something never before performed, it gives one a feeling of achievement and success. After my husband's stroke, I taught myself to use a riding lawn mower by using the manual. (Sometimes you have to face some of the same difficulties if your spouse becomes disabled). Until the steps were familiar, the written instructions remained in my shirt pocket. There was an overwhelming sense of pride experienced until I saw a little boy with shoulders about a foot wide driving a big John Deere tractor in the field next to my yard. Both widows and widowers have their own unique set of difficulties to face; however with patience and courage the job that lies before them will be successful.

SOLUTIONS THAT BRING ON THE ADJUSTMENT PERIOD

Bear in mind that reaching the adjustment period will be like climbing a mountain and all survivors will not reach the top of the mountain at the same time. Take note of the following solutions that will contribute to the adjustment period, which is the goal of all grief survivors.

TRUST IN GOD. First, trust in God. He will never leave you nor abandon you as Jesus said, "I am with you alway even to the end of the world" (Matt. 28:20). Jesus cares when you are sorrowful and wants to heal the broken heart of a soul that has suffered the loss of a spouse. God offers comfort to the Hebrews stating, "I will in no wise fail thee, neither will I in anywise forsake thee. So with good courage we say, the Lord is my helper, I will not fear: What can man do unto me?" (Heb. 13:5-6).

Pray. Pray often for God's help, comfort, and guidance. "Evening, and morning; and at noon, will I pray, and cry aloud; and he shall hear my voice" (Psm. 55:17). Enlisting the Lord's help is essential in meeting our daily stresses and the challenging troubles which try our souls. The inspired writer declares, "Is any among you afflicted (suffering)? Let him pray" (James 5:13). David cries, "Cast thy burden upon the Lord, and he shall sustain thee" (Psm. 55:22). Peter writes: "Casting all your care upon him, for he careth for you" (1 Peter 5:7). Peter's soothing words provided comfort and strength for Christians long ago, and further if we will turn our troubles to Him, the same peace will come.

Find Comfort From God's Word. If your spouse was a Christian, it will provide great comfort during the adjustment period. The child of God has that sustainable ingredient in Christ called hope that allows the believer to cling to the promises of God. Peter writes, "The Lord is not slack concerning his promise," (2 Peter 3:9) which suggests the promises of God are sure, certain, and reliable (Heb. 9:15, 10:36). Paul writes, "But I would not have you to be ignorant, brethren, concerning them which are asleep, that he sorrow not, even as others which have no hope. For if we believe that Jesus died and rose again, even so them also which sleep in Jesus will God bring with him" (1 Thess. 4:13-18).

The blessed assurance of God is the result of those who live in accordance to God's Word as the promise extends beyond the grave. When Lazarus died, Jesus told Mary and Martha that their brother shall rise again (John 11:23). John, the apostle of love, said, "Blessed are the dead which die in the Lord from henceforth; yea saith the spirit, that they may rest from their labors and their works do follow them" (Rev. 14:13). David, the man after God's own heart, said, "Precious in the sight of the Lord is the death of his saints" (Psm. 116:15). Read the following Scriptures that offer hope and comfort (Phil. 1:21; Rom. 15:4; 1 Cor. 10:13; 1 Peter 1:3-4; John 14:1-3; Rev. 14:13). One of my favorite passages in the Bible comes from John, "And God shall wipe away all tears from their eyes; and there shall be no more death, neither sorrow, nor crying, neither shall there be any more pain" (Rev. 21:4). The child of God has that sustainable gift, hope, which comes through the promises that God has made to the faithful (2 Peter 3:9; Heb. 6:15; 9:15; 10:23).

Heavenly Reunion. The Bible teaches us there will be a heavenly reunion with our loved ones, who have gone home to be with the Lord. Jesus assured His disciples, "I go to prepare a place for you and if I go and prepare a place for you, I will come again, and receive you to myself; that where I am, there ye may be also" (John 14:2-3). This heavenly home comes without regard to cost or price, as the redeemed will continue throughout the endless ages. Remember what David said following the death of his infant son? "But now that he is dead, wherefore should I fast? Can I bring him back again, I shall go to him, but he shall not return to me" (2 Sam. 12:23). David knew only what the heavenly Father revealed to him and he was certain there would be a home for all those that prepared to go there. What a glorious day and what a grand reunion that will be.

Continue To Worship. A grief survivor, transcending any other period of distress, must remain constant in their faithfulness to the Creator. There is no substitute for assembling with Christians to worship. We have seen surviving spouses that could not bring themselves to return to their place in worship to almighty God. In the beginning it may be difficult with all the memories and recollections experienced, but brothers and sisters in Christ will embrace you with love and the deepest concern for you. If it becomes necessary some grieving spouses find it too difficult to bear, and thus attend a sister congregation where the pain will not be as great. Remember, it is in the assembly where God's children gather collectively to worship and draw strength from one another. The writer to the Hebrews, declares, "Not forsaking the assembling of yourselves together, as the manner of some is; but exhorting one another: and so much the more, as you see the day approaching" (Heb. 10:25).

Reach Out To Others. Surviving spouses need all the companionship with friends and loved ones that is possible. You need their love and encouragement more than ever. The Hebrew writer urged, "Let us consider one another to provoke unto love and good works" (Heb. 10:24). Christians were to provoke, or "stir-up" one another to love and good works. This would clearly show reaching out to draw strength from Christians as well as children of God returning the same care and concern for those recovering from a devastating loss.

Concentrate On Good Memories. Ponder and concentrate on the good memories you shared with your mate, instead of lingering on your loss. Think of the children your spouse helped you parent and all the memories from which you may draw. Someone has said that thieves and robbers can steal everything we posses, but he cannot take away your precious memories (Prov. 10: 7; 1 Cor. 15:2). It will be difficult for surviving spouses, but strive to go forward. Your loved one would want you to continue and to make the best of your life. As a spouse I know it is difficult but we must persevere to do our best and make a positive contribution with our lives. Resign yourself to the unchangeable. Only then will our hearts begin to heal.

TOPICS FOR DISCUSSION

1. What is the cruelest feature of a spouse deprived of their mate?

2. What is the most difficult adjustment to make in accepting the loss of a spouse?

3. How important is the role of the church to help widows and widowers reach the adjustment period?

4. What can I do individually to help a spouse that has lost a mate?

BRIEF BIOGRAPHY OF AVIS C. CORLEY

Avis Corley, born on September 26, 1936. She married Preston Porter on December 20, 1953, where they engaged in full-time work with churches of Christ from 1953-1992. They had two sons, Adrian and Randall. Randall, the youngest, died of an accident a week before his 19th birthday in 1979. She has three grandchildren and one great-grandchild. The first great-grandchild was stillborn in 2001. Her husband experienced a stroke and eventually died of heart failure on July 25, 2000. Avis was a compassionate caregiver for about eight years.

Avis is a prolific writer having her poetry and articles published in many church publications. Many of her writings and poetry have become translated in the language of India. She has taught many children and ladies Bible classes, while giving poetry readings of her original poems. She is a retired library assistant. She is a member of the Pine Bluff church of Christ in Toccopola, MS. Her address is: Avis C. Porter, 9803 Highway 336, Thaxton, MS 38871-9711. (Thanks Avis for your wonderful contribution to this literary effort– Bob Spurlin).

Chapter Five

When Faced
With The
Loss Of A Child

5

Many duties and responsibilities come to the gospel preacher. Preaching sermons, teaching classes, conducting home Bible studies, and visiting the sick, the shut-ins, and other jobs that we cannot pass to others. One of the happiest responsibilities for the preacher is conducting wedding ceremonies while the most difficult chore is preaching memorial services, which we recognize as a funeral. This preacher has conducted probably hundreds of memorial services and each one is different with some being believers while others are unbelievers. There are many other differences that make a memorial service unique within itself and needs special care in providing comfort and strength to the surviving family. During and after the memorial service this preacher inquired from surviving spouses, "What was your greatest loss?" The loss of a "spouse" (husband or wife) or the loss of a "child?" Most of the time the question asked, and the answer echoed from the hearts of grieving people said, "The loss of my child is the most devastating event and the greatest to overcome than any other event experienced."

A PERSONAL STORY

During my tenure as a preacher of the gospel a collection of thoughts and events has provided me with valuable insights about the loss of a child. This writer can only speak from personal experience and the loss of a child to my wife and me has been overwhelming and at times engulfed us. Fortunately the loss of the spouse has never visited me and for which I am most thankful. There are no scientific polling data to offer the reader about this matter, but a few thoughts have come to mind. First, a child that dies before his parents is an unnatural act. It is an expected and inescapable conclusion that children of parents have the responsibility at the proper time to bury their parents. Otherwise, it defies the laws of nature. Second, our children are part of our bodies and that makes them, "Bone of my bones and flesh of my flesh" (Gen. 2:23). This, of course, would be especially true with the mother of the child. We often forget the mother carries the child within her body for nine months before the delivery comes to pass. The connection between child and mother cannot be questioned. The fathers' linkage between the son and daughter is a strong bond between each other, but cannot compare with that of the mother. Nonetheless the union between parent and child is enormously close and secure, which is undeniable. If you were a parent, how would you describe the bond that exists with your son or daughter? This is a subject so often relegated to the unimportant, but to lovers of truth recognized as a fact in basis.

We must not blame God for all our ills in life. My precious daughter suffered death at the hands of a reckless driver, and some people responded, "It is God's will." My family and this writer do not accept the inclination that it was God's will, or that God was at fault at such a crushing nightmare. My wife and I uncovered limited information about the accident taking our daughter's life. From eyewitness accounts we became aware of the driver of the furniture truck exceeding the speed limit that caused the impact of our daughter's car causing the accident. We had the opportunity to meet and talk with the passenger in the furniture truck some weeks later after the accident. With candor and courage he admitted that he and the driver were talking fluently when suddenly our daughter's car appeared before them. The speed, coupled with taking their eyes off the road for a split-second, caused the accident. Reader friends, can you imagine the God of heaven sitting on His majestic throne causing terrible accidents to occur, inflicting disease, hardship, or other forms of trial whenever the mood strikes Him? If true, what a deliberate and calculating God we serve.

SIX STEPS IN GRIEVING FORMULA

Many of us who describe ourselves as grief survivors recognize we are not alone in this painful experience. Losing a child puts us in an exclusive club. As stated earlier such a loss is an unnatural act and one unexpected. Christians cannot become immunized against this painful event of suffering. The writer of Job states, "Man that is born of woman is of few days, and full of trouble" (Job 14:1). We have discovered over a period of time, through our painful experience, that six steps exist in the grieving formula:

1. **Shock.** One is stunned beyond feeling as the announced news simply does not register in the mind. Rather like the computer that does not recognize the command given to it. When the County Coroner and state trooper rang the door bell, the information came with clarity, but this father of a sixteen year old daughter could not calculate or analyze the information. Several individuals had gathered in our home moments after announcing our daughter's death, and they saw a man in a wheelchair without emotion, tears, or any likeness of responding to such devastating information.

2. **Denial.** This step is a progression in the formula of accepting and dealing with such a crushing announcement. This step is a rejection and total defiance of the untimely death of our child. My wife and I slowly moved through the shock stage to the denial phase. We could not accept the news as we were becoming more emotional and in denial.

3. **Disbelief.** Rejecting this disaster by refusing it .

occurred is the outgrowth of denying that it ever happened. Jacob wept with disbelief at the news of his son, Joseph's death (Gen. 37:31-35). Jacob's sons deceived their father and the depth of grief and disbelief was overwhelming. This step in the grieving formula, as with the other steps, cannot come by a timetable.

4. **Blame.** Such stress of losing a child often causes the surviving parents and other family members to place blame on someone. The day our daughter suffered a fatal auto accident, a separating of the spirit from the body began the blame game (James 2:26). The practice of the blame game is an endless cycle in it's effort to bring some justification to suffering families. Some have consistently placed blame on God, even in times of trial (James 1:13).

5. **Momentary management**–As this timeless journey continues over the symbolic hills and valleys of adjusting to the loss of a child, our goal of reaching the plateau of adjustment will continue. Momentary management includes the formula of coping with occasional relapses, which often come before reaching the adjustment stage. This step comes with slips and momentary falls that show we have not achieved our goal. My wife and I have felt items under control when suddenly a smell, song, a piece of clothing worn by our daughter, or some other material item would cause endless sobbing. This is a necessary step if we would reach the next level.

6. **Adjustment.** When we have reached this period of acceptance and come to grips with the loss of a child, most believe the hurt and pain will go in a protected place in our consciousness. This parent, who still grieves for his daughter, will not state in a clear fashion that sorrow and grief will no longer be in your life. Almost eight years have passed since our daughter passed from this earthly pilgrimage to the immortal shore of Paradise. Let us stress the adjustment period will be constant and recurring. The normal response when talking with those who have lost a loved one, "Time is the best healer and with the passing of time one will come to accept this loss." These words may ring hollow, but with the slow passing of time He can be a healer of our souls. Christians must never lose heart and remember that we have a friend in Jesus (John 15:14-15).

THOUGHTS BY AVIS C. PORTER

When you first receive the news that your child was dead, it is almost overwhelming. You are too stunned for words. You may then cry out with great anguish to God. As a parent, the general rule is that we are "supposed" to perish before our child. Our son or daughter's life separated by death will change our lives forever. This separation is for the rest of your earthly life, which makes this nearly impossible to bear. But with the Lord's help, you will be able to endure it. Since the beginning of time parents have faced this terrible loss, and so will you (Gen. 4:1-26).

I once asked a mother, who lost her son in the

war, how she was able to tolerate such loss? She said, "You just bear with it." After a drunk driver killed my oldest brother, 25 years old, in an auto accident, someone asked my Daddy how he could stand it. Daddy replied, "How can you not stand it?" It would be my fondest wish for you and me to recover from such grief, and the adjustment will follow. If you sever your arm and joining it was not possible, you will never get over it, but will make the change and life will continue. When the loss of your child comes, life will continue, but a part of you will die forever. You'll always long for the way it used to be while you are on earth, which is the way it was with your child. So long as life continues and there is a soundness of mind, you will always have a longing for your child. To give your deceased child one last hug and one more kiss; to hear the sound of his/her voice, to hear his/her laughter, and to be with him/her again would be priceless. (Parents, if you still have your children, learn the lesson from those of us that can no longer have human contact with our child).

After I lost my son, a friend who had lost her son years earlier said, "It gets easier to bear in time." I have found that to be true and more so as the years have passed. As a mother I believe it is the worst possible pain to endure on earth. When you go through such an unbearable period, you will meet any obstacle that may come, because nothing could exceed the most difficult time of your life. Someday, you will be able to learn from your experience and help others by comforting them who have endured such misfortune.

TOPICS FOR DISCUSSION

1. Why is the loss of a child considered to be the most difficult challenge to bear?

2. How useful is it to play the "Blame game" in coping with the loss of a child?

3. How would you respond to the notion that suffering the loss of a child is God's will?

4. What will help grieving parents to reach the adjustment state with the loss of their child?

Chapter Six

When Faced With A Bedridden Existence

The author of this book for almost eight years has waged a battle against the dreaded disease, multiple sclerosis. Dramatic changes in life style have been a shock that affects the entire family. This writer has always been active as an evangelist, father, and husband for about thirty-three years. My devotion to my loved ones and commitment to my work has been the center of my life. However, we are aware of countless others who have to endure even more in their daily existence. As a child the old expression, "woe is me," which suggested the difficulties and trials that one was experiencing has become real. This shows that if we look around, we will always discover those that are in a more serious circumstance. What is the correct formula for dealing with those who are hurting, dealing with a dreaded disease, coping with the loss of a loved one, or confined to bed? Jesus came into a world that was hurting and sick at heart. He is the Great Physician and will deal with whatever needs we might have. The Savior was eating with the publicans and sinners as the Pharisees began to murmur, "Why do ye eat and drink with the publicans and sinners? And Jesus answered and said, they that are whole need not a physician, but they that are sick. I came not to call the righteous, but sinners to repentance" (Luke 5:30-31). Jesus, the Great Physician, can heal the human heart and cure the ills that inflict the mass of humanity (Matt. 4:23).

LOSS OF DIGNITY

Oh, how often we forget the everyday blessings of waking up, showering, getting dressed, going to work and providing for our family as a normal life style. Exchanging love for our families while using every opportunity to serve our fellowman in service to God is the purpose of our existence. After being told that you are ill with progressive multiple sclerosis and to face a bedridden existence is a shock that defies human description. When in its grip, the disease began to spread and caused extreme weakness in my lower extremities and on my right side. These symptoms became disturbing to say the least. The most difficult challenge to face was the dependence on my wife and other family members for the most basic care. Some of the most cherished moments experienced was our family coming together to eat our meals combined with all the stories and anecdotes that made it so enjoyable. Now, dependent for my meals, given a simple glass of water, and bathed by family members were just the beginning in my care. From the start having these simple tasks done was humiliating and embarrassing while feeling helpless as an infant. "This should not happen to me," I would say! It happens to others and they must bear that burden, not me! One can become consumed with the day-by-day confinement to a hospital bed. However, seeing the seriousness of this condition demands a positive attitude.

LORD FORGIVE ME WHEN I WHINE
Today, upon a bus,
I saw a lovely girl with golden hair,
I envied her...She seemed so happy...
and I wished I were as fair.
When suddenly she rose to leave,
I saw her hobble down the aisle;
She had one leg and used a crutch;
but as she passed...a smile!
Oh GOD, forgive me when I whine,
I have two good legs.
The world is mine.

I stopped to buy some candy.
The boy who sold it had such charm.
I talked with him. He seemed so glad.
If I were late, 'twould do no harm.
And as I left he said to me,
"thank you."
You have been so kind.
It's nice to talk with folks like you.
For you see, he said, "I'm blind."

Oh, GOD forgive me when I whine,
I have two eyes. The world is mine.

Later, while walking down the street,
I saw a child with eyes so blue.
He stood and watched the others play.
He did not know what to do.
I stopped a moment, then I said,
"why don't you join the others, dear?"
He look ahead without a word,
and then I knew he could not hear.
Oh, GOD forgive me when I whine,
I have two ears. The world is mine.

With feet to take me where I'd go,
With eyes to see the sunset's glow,
With ears to hear what I should know...
Oh, GOD forgive me when I whine.
You have truly blessed me.
The world is mine...
~ Author Unknown

ANGER AGAINST GOD

Suffering a bedridden existence is the most difficult challenge that one can endure. Far too many want to place blame and show anger against God, which is an empty exercise. While preaching in a gospel meeting in East Tennessee there was a man that was angry against God. His son had escaped dismemberment or any serious injury while he was serving in the Vietnam War. This father was so thrilled to have his son home and in one piece that he was beside himself. Unfortunately, the son worked for Tennessee Power, Inc. The first day on-the-job he was climbing a power pole when he accidentally suffered death by grabbing a live wire that contained thousands of volts of electricity. "Where was God when my son died," the father said to the preacher? The preacher replied, "He was at the same place when they killed his son." Playing the blame game is always easy and disparages God for death, illness, taxes, and a bedridden existence. James, the brother of our Lord, said, "Blessed is the man that endureth temptation (or trials), for when he is tried, he shall receive the crown of life, which the Lord hath promised to them that love him. Let no man say when he is tempted (trials), I am tempted of God, for God cannot be tempted with evil, neither tempteth he any man" (James 1:12-13).

We must not blame God for all our ills in life. My precious daughter suffered death at the hands of a reckless driver, and then people responded, "It is God's will." My family and this writer do not accept the inclination that it was God's will, or that God was at fault at such a crushing nightmare. Reader friends, can you imagine the God of heaven sitting on his majestic throne causing terrible accidents to occur, inflicting disease, hardship, or other forms of trial whenever the mood strikes him? Have we forgotten the story of Job in the Old Testament? It was Satan that subjected Job and his family to the misfortune inflicted on them, not God (Job 1:8-22). The patriarch,

Job, did not batter his breast and blame God for his ills. He recognized the source of his problems and it was Satan. Paul in the New Testament stated to the Corinthians, "Lest Satan should get an advantage of us, for we are not ignorant of his devices" (2 Cor. 2:11). Paul was warning the Christians at Corinth that we should not be ignorant of Satan's tactics. Subsequently, many tools are in the arsenal of Satan that can assault and victimize us at will. Suffering in all its forms and compositions can alter our thinking and sway us in our judgment and decision making. What is the real clue or glimmer of hope?

HOLD TO AN UNSHAKEABLE FAITH

Scores of people enduring a bedfast condition are desperately seeking treatment that would ease our physical, emotional, and spiritual health. Reaching out for any cure that may reduce the pain and discomfort they suffer is the goal of all of us that endure a disabled state. This author has received countless offers for treatment and drugs from well-meaning people who have our best interest at heart. So many facing this incredible test are desperate and will reach out for anything that might bring hope. We should never lose sight of an unshakable faith that will help us during the difficulties that affect our lives.

If all the suffering and hardship Job endured was not enough, Satan charged the Lord that his servant would curse him to the face if his flesh were smitten. The Lord said to Satan, "Behold, he is in thine hand; but save his life" (Job 2:6). This faithful man of God faced a crisis with sore boils from the foot to the crown of his head. The pain was so great and intense that "he sat down among the ashes" (Job 2:8). For the first time Job's wife speaks saying: "Dost thou still retain thine own integrity? Curse God, and die" (Job 2: 9). Job's strength was in God and regardless of what his wife said, his loyalty to God would not waver despite his wife's wishes. Job was not one to "ask why," but answered his wife, "Thou speakest as one of the foolish women speaketh. What? Shall we receive good at the hand of God, and shall we not receive evil? In all this did not Job sin with his lips" (Job 2:10). If we receive good and positive blessings, may we question God and ask why, when evil visits our door? Job's spiritual compass would not falter with his anchor solidly embedded in the rock of ages. The patriarch's wife, his friends, loss of property, livestock, and the loss of all his children would not shake his faith in Jehovah. When misfortune and heartache strikes at our door let us remember Job and his unshakable faith in God. The victory that we hope to achieve comes with an unfailing faith in Almighty God. John writes, "And this is the victory that overcometh the world, even our faith" (1 John 5:4).

PRACTICAL ITEMS TO DO

Hope versus despair and true solidarity seems shaky at best when faced with a bedridden existence. Whatever form of distress we may be facing, we can endure it and reach the mountaintop. Hope through Christ is the first step we must take (John 14: 6). It is much like the doctor who gives a thorough examination and asks a series of questions that will give him our family history. It may seem tedious and time consuming, yet this is the only way he can reach an accurate diagnosis. Jesus, the Great Physician, knows his patient and is aware of our physical and spiritual disorder. Overcoming distress can be therapeutic which includes reaching out to others. This writer has discovered over many years that one can overcome such depression by having contact with others. We do not disparage the enormous challenge that one has with a bedridden existence. Yet, many have discovered that their problems are not nearly as bad as they previously thought.

As one suffering confinement for nearly eight years, nothing gets me charged-up more than receiving cards, notes, and letters written by the individual. Start writing a journal or book of your life that tells of your remarkable experiences. Good times and bad will give a clear and panoramic view of your life. Beginning such a task may be difficult, but it is a growing exercise and the final product will go to my family and we hope to succeeding generations. This exercise is therapeutic and healthy, and will provide mental and spiritual growth. Christ is the solution and satisfies every need that we have (Luke 5:30-31). God will not overwhelm us with such tasks that we cannot endure (1 Cor. 10:13). Our Father in heaven always provides a way out, if we are willing to look for it. We would not presume to suggest that these ides would remove the disease that has caused a bedridden existence. We do believe that drawing closer to God will provide the encouragement needed in times of great difficulty. Reader friends, good luck in your search to find peace and endure to the end (Rev. 2:10).

TOPICS FOR DISCUSSION

1. What is the formula in coping with a bedridden existence?

2. The loss of one's dignity is a great challenge—what can we do to lift his/her spirits?

3. How futile is it to show anger to God, or our loved ones during such confinement?

4. What are some practical items that can help the bedridden patient? As Christians what can we do?

Chapter Seven

Challenges To All Caregivers

7

Webster's Collegiate Dictionary defines caregiver, "concerned about or extend care, to feel interest or concern, to give care for the sick." In short the "caregiver" is the life and blood for the one receiving care. Caregivers that offer their time and energy while denying themselves of life's basic pleasures should come to realize the tremendous sacrifice they make to their love one. Several years ago the American people learned that President Ronald Reagan contracted the Alzheimer's disease. This was a shock to the nation as sympathy was far-reaching in its concern for the former president and the devastating disease, which he suffered. The former First Lady, Nancy Reagan, was in need of encouragement and empathy as she faced the biggest hurdle of her life. Family members began to speak-up informing the American people of the all-consuming task and dedication of the former first lady in her care of the president.

This illustration only serves to keep us knowledgeable of the countless unsung heroes that give the care and compassion to their loved one, who is suffering with a terminal or devastating disease. As a preacher for some 30 years it has been my pleasure to visit the sick and shut-ins often. Many of these find themselves confined because of their physical abnormality and illnesses that make such necessary. Many family members and friends often forget the wife, husband, mother, father and those providing the primary care for their loved ones. The caregiver faces 168 hours a week in seeing to the necessary duties and at times mundane tasks for the loved one. Dropping by for a short visit, shaking the hand of the shut-in, and extending a token "howdy" to the caregiver doesn't relieve one from their duty to the shut-in and caregiver. We are all busy and most have family duties, jobs and other time-consuming responsibilities. Let us be aware of the Golden Rule stated by the Lord Himself. Jesus said, "Therefore all things whatsoever ye would that men should do to you, to ye even so to them: for this is the law and the prophets" (Matt. 7:12). We could easily spend an hour or so relieving the "caregiver" and let him or her get out to relax for a while. They might enjoy having a meal or visiting with other Christians, which would give a real "shot in the arm" and rejuvenate them as well as lifting their spirits. This writer has seen this done regularly as the church, mindful of this need, will assign volunteers to give the caregiver a periodic break freeing them with some rest and recreation. This .

will not only give the caregiver a much-needed pause from their task, but will give us the opportunity to visit and become aware of the lifestyle of the shut-in. Let us remember the words of Paul, "As we have therefore opportunity, let us do good unto all men, especially unto them who are of the household of faith" (Gal. 6:10). We must be opportunity conscious and you have my promise that great satisfaction and contentment will swell your heart with gladness.

OBSERVATIONS FROM A SHUT-IN

My beloved wife, Beverly, and I married on July 17, 1971. We served the Lord's church in various places throughout the southeastern part of our country. The arrival of a son and daughter made our family complete. Despite the good times and bad, we were a happy foursome. This preacher happened to come along when local congregations were not compensating the preacher in a financial way that would make life comfortable. Nonetheless we never felt deprived of the essentials and loved the work that we did in spreading the good news to a lost world. Beverly was always the best wife and mother that a man could possibly want. When we would decide to leave a place and move elsewhere more times than not the church would give us a "going away party." Consistently, many Christians would say, "Bob, you go along and leave if you like, but Beverly and the kids are staying with us!" This preacher would respond, "We are a package deal, and where I go, they go." We were always a close family and through it all we stuck together like glue.

Little did we know that before our twenty-fifth anniversary Beverly and I would discover her husband would become diagnosed with multiple sclerosis? Compounded with that shocking news, four days later our beautiful daughter, Bethany, would suffer a fatal automobile accident. Even though we both suffered a devastating loss when our daughter suddenly perished by an automobile accident, my beloved wife and caregiver had to begin providing daily care for her husband. We both wept together and sobbed as we tried to cope with the loss of our daughter. My wife, although grieving, was unceasing in her role as a "caregiver" to a husband suffering with such a progressive disease as multiple sclerosis. Together we studied our Bibles and discussed God's word and in time our convictions were proven correct that faithful Christians would go into paradise (Luke 23:42-43). Beverly was the "sole breadwinner" teaching second-grade, which is no small chore and traveling twenty-five miles round-trip doubled the fatigue when she would return home in the afternoon. (In July of 2001, we were able to make a move enabling Beverly to be five minutes from school).

During the early stages of this crippling disease my father was conscientious in seeing needs met. The first few years of this battle against MS my father would transport me to the doctors, bath me, and supplied whatever need was necessary. My wife is no longer able to lift me, therefore my family: Jere, Calvin, and my son, Paul would drop by at their convenience to bath me. It became necessary for my father to suspend any lifting of me, because of his open-heart (bypass) surgery, but during the early years of my confinement his help was indispensable. Summarizing, it has been a family affair in my personal care, but my beautiful wife has been the constancy of my support and the lifter of my spirits. This prejudiced shut-in has seen my chief caregiver daily and she rarely, if ever, complains although she has every reason to do so.

EVALUATING MY CAREGIVER

This shut-in can only speak for himself, but there are times when my pain, discomfort, and stress will be more than one can bear. To hear those say that he or she has never complained about being sick or shut-in is questionable having visited such individuals over a thirty-year period as a minister of the gospel. Such an attitude defies soundness of logic. It seems that at times all members of the human family would have a weak moment and would express some negative thoughts. This preacher can only say that it has been my objective to keep such complaints and negative thoughts at a minimum. My caregiver, in the backdrop of the last eight years, has faced various obstacles in handling the disappointments and regrets linked to such a disease. My caregiver has been able to handle the peaks and valleys with great faith and courage. She is able to take the most unpleasant and challenging circumstance and transform it to an experience of hope and stability. As much as possible in coping with this particular disease, my caregiver makes such an existence manageable. Her glowing presence, enchanting smile, and lifting of my spirits gets me through one day at a time. Yes, my caregiver is the hero of my life, my wife—Beverly.

OBSERVATIONS FROM THE CAREGIVER

Putting together the material in this book made it necessary to call on various people for advice and input. This chapter addresses the subject of caregivers and the single caregiver that I know best in the world is my personal caregiver, Beverly–my wife. My wife composed the material below and her analysis and deep feelings on the subject adds much to this section. She is my sunshine and the apple of my eye and always makes my day a little brighter. Thanks, Beverly, for faithfully standing by my side during this time of challenge.

The care of my shut-in: My husband, rarely complains to his caregiver, however I know his pain and discomfort is greater than he expresses. I can sense it in his eyes and face with each passing day. We have been a couple for nearly thirty-three years as husband and wife and to see your spouse confined to bed is difficult to grasp. One day he was healthy, active, and energetic in all of his duties. The preacher conducting our wedding ceremony so long ago asked us to repeat the vows, "For better or worse, in sickness and in health." Those vows meant something to me and in good or bad times this spouse and caregiver provides the care needed for my husband's daily existence.

A caregiver misses the joy of being a couple. Going to a restaurant to get "carry out orders" for my husband and me to eat, does not begin to substitute for sitting together enjoying a good meal and exchanging conversation with each other. While waiting on the meal preparation this caregiver could not help but look around and see other couples sitting together, glazing at each other with love, and only wishing that it was my husband and I.

One of the joys missed is the physical intimacy with my bedridden husband. There are many basics included in the marriage union: (1) emotional, (2) spiritual, and (3) physical. Each ingredient is of equal importance and the caregiver must learn to cope with the insufficiency and absence of the needs unfulfilled because of the invalid state of the spouse. There are many fundamental items that one can do to compensate for those because of a disabled state. Giving reassurance and comforting words of love will fill the emptiness normally taken for granted. Paul writes, "So ought men to love their wives as their own bodies; He that loveth his wife loveth himself" (Eph. 5:28). Wives have an equal responsibility to their husband to love them as they would their own bodies. The closest physical bond known between those in the human family is the husband-wife union; it is little wonder that God used this union to describe the intimacy between Christ and His church.

My spouse was always willing to help me with projects connected to my job in the school where I work. This caregiver misses the instances where my husband would read a story to a group of students asking and answering questions of the children. His skill as a communicator and preacher served him well in such tasks mentioned. The last time he took part in such occasions was in his wheelchair and the students were so engaged in the story that being in a disabled state was of no concern to them. Some of my second graders still ask about my husband and what his condition is like.

As a caregiver taking care of my spouse has been a duty fully accepted knowing that he would do the same for me if my health declined. So often, reflection is made on our trips that we made as a family to the Great Smoky Mountain national park, Yellowstone, or just visiting friends that we have known in past years. Those trips were so memorable and filled with exciting and remarkable events that they have become permanently etched in our memory and will never fade away.

For nearly eight years multiple sclerosis devastated my spouse with a disease that has altered our lives forever. The first twenty-five years of our marriage my husband was a partner and willingly helped me as a preacher's wife in so many ways that challenged us both. He was willing to perform household duties like vacuuming, washing the dishes, mopping the floors, and often would manage the washer and drier. My spouse never felt superior when aiding me with domestic duties in the house, or chores outside with mowing and manicuring the lawn, helping me with planting fruit trees or flowers. All of these joint efforts brought us even closer together.

These are some of my memories and thoughts about my life as a caregiver. There will always be ups and downs for all married couples and this wife and caregiver feels blessed that she can still exchange memories with her husband that only we can share together. We will never give-up, but keep persevering regardless of the difficulties that visit us from day-to-day. Paul writes, "I can do all things through Christ, which strengthenth me" (Phil. 4:13).

TOPICS FOR DISCUSSION

1. What is the definition of a "caregiver" and what characteristics should they possess?

2. What can we do to relief the stress that the "caregivers" face in their daily lives?

3. Humor is essential in the daily interaction between shut-in and caregiver. Discuss Solomon's statement, "A merry heart doeth good like medicine?" (Prov. 17:22)

Chapter Eight

When Facing Loneliness

8

Webster's Collegiate Dictionary defines the word loneliness, "the quality or state of being lonely or lonesome." Who has not faced such a condition at some point in their lives? Nearly eight years of confinement because of a crippling disease, multiple sclerosis, has produced periods of loneliness. Such is not surprising or unpredictable considering the nature of the disease. However, anyone experiencing physical disabilities is not the only one to experience loneliness. This condition can come to those that face stress on the job, family problems, and financial difficulties. Those that are lonely often reach misery and hopelessness defying description, but this is not an incurable condition.

Whether we would like to agree with it or not, loneliness is a universal problem. It visits every human soul at some time in every culture, every race, every class, every age, and in human history. It is inescapable, and has expressed itself throughout the ages in music, literature and art. To feel lonely is to join the rest of humanity in recognizing that we are somehow fundamentally separated from each other, doomed to speak and yet never fully understood. Not only is loneliness broad in scope, it also comes with a host of different emotions. People who feel lonely describe it as painful combined with strong feelings of depression, suicide, aggression, and low regard of themselves. Being lonely for too long may not be good. And while we suffer a wandering existence, we are social beings, needing each other, to bond, to connect, to love (Heb. 13:1). It is the problem of human existence to seek or fill a need that can never come to resolution, to fill the vacuum of loneliness in our lives.

So what is loneliness? Is it a feeling? A condition? For different people, it can have different effects. It is hard to describe exactly what it is, or how we come to feel this way. Perhaps a better question is "what is loneliness for you?" We encourage you to read the following information about loneliness, the various forms, causes and the ways that people cope with loneliness.

POTPOURRI OF INFO ON LONELINESS

Loneliness is not necessarily being alone. We may be alone for long periods without feeling at all lonely. On the other hand we may feel lonely in a familiar setting without understanding why. The best way to understand loneliness is to examine some of the ways people experience it. You may feel lonely when:

• You are alone and you don't feel you have a choice not to be;

• You feel that you're lacking attachments you had in the past;

• You are facing changes in your life–loss of spouse, child, job, moving to new a place;

• You feel there's no one in your life with whom you can share your feelings and experiences;

• Your awareness is that you're unacceptable, unlovable, and not worthwhile even if others don't share those observations.

MISCONCEPTIONS ABOUT LONELINESS

Loneliness is more powerful by what you say it means. Scores of individuals are susceptible to the following misconceptions about loneliness:

• "Loneliness is a sign of weakness, or immaturity."

• "There's something wrong with me if I'm lonely. These should be the best years of my life."

• "I'm the only one who feels this way."

If you believe these misconceptions you may believe that loneliness results from a failing in your personality. Research suggests that those who think of loneliness as a flaw have the following difficulties:

• Greater difficulty in taking on social settings, in asserting themselves, in making phone calls to open social contact, in introducing themselves to others, by taking part in groups, and enjoying themselves with others.

• Difficulty with groups, and feeling out of place in social get-togethers.

• Less skill in admission, less responsive to others, and a greater tendency to approach social gatherings with suspicion and mistrust.

• More likelihood of evaluating themselves and others in negative terms and more tendencies to expect others to reject them.

People experiencing loneliness often feel depressed, angry, afraid, and misunderstood. They often become critical of themselves, excessively sensitive, showing self-pity, or becoming critical of others.

When these instances occur, loneliness takes place, which self-perpetuates this condition. Some become discouraged, lose their sense of need and motivation to interact with other groups of people. Many will isolate themselves from people. Others will deal with loneliness by becoming too quickly involved with people without evaluating the effects. They may later find themselves unhealthy with others producing deeper problems than before.

WHAT CAN HELP ME
TO OVERCOME LONELINESS

Count Your Many Blessings. David summarizes the greatness of God with his creative handiwork and the special role that man plays (Psalms 8:3-5). It is breathtaking to consider all the Lord has given to man, which demands a heart full of thanksgiving. The man after God's on heart, said: "Blessed be the Lord, who daily loadeth us with benefits, even the God of our salvation" (Psm. 68:19). To overcome loneliness involves counting our blessings; discounting our blessings spells pessimism. The wonderful old hymn sums it up like this: "Count your many blessings, name them one by one. Count your many belssings see what God hath done."

Jacob knew how to count his blessings. When Esau "lifted his eyes, and saw the women and the children; and said, Who are those with thee? And he said, the children which God hath graciously given thy servant" (Gen. 33:5). Jacob urged Esau to take the gift he offered. "Take, I pray thee, my blessing that is brought to thee; because God hath dealt graciously with me, and because I have enough. And he urged him, and he took it" (Gen. 33:11). As Christians, the blessings of God includes not only the material, but also with the spiritual blessings (Eph. 1:3). As a Christian I am blessed with forgiveness from the Lord. "Blessed are they whose iniquities are forgiven, and whose sins are covered" (Rom. 4:7). God's blessings will secure the lonely heart and uphold us in times of loneliness.

Cast All Our Cares On The Lord. There are times when loneliness and stress can become overwhelming. Paul, the apostle, pressed and perplexed, endured problems on every side and continued to reach for the heavens (2 Cor. 4:8-11). We can allow the pressures of life to consume us, wallowing in self-pity and paralyzed with inaction. Or, like Paul and Silas, we can choose another course by recognizing God as the solution to my problems. Peter writes: "Casting all your care upon Him; for He careth for you" (1 Peter 5:7). In exchange for my cares, my Maker "will fill (my) mouth with laughing and (my) lips with rejoicing" (Job. 8:21). Those despondent and lonely may take comfort from God: "For the Lord taketh pleasure in his people: he will beautify the meek with salvation. Let the saints be joyful in glory: let them sing aloud upon their beds" (Psm. 149:4-5).

Those buried in loneliness will be overcome with a negative attitude. If a person believes he will fail, regardless of the objective before him, such failure will without a doubt occur (Prov. 23:7). One consumed by negativism and pessimism by his attitude will fail before beginning. Most individuals surrendering to pessimism will never overcome loneliness. He who ignores the "burning bridges" before he gets to them will never successfully get to the other side. How tragic to see those suffering from loneliness, which makes the smallest task seem insurmountable. We see the problem with the ten spies who gave a bad report of Canaan to Israel (Num. 13:27-33).

The negative attitude questions God and His goodness with doubt. His strength will lift us up in times of anguish. People who have a positive outlook on life succeed far more than those who look at life through rose-colored glasses. God wants us to fill our minds and hearts with wholesome thoughts that give us a positive outlook on life and make us better people. Paul writes: "Finally, brethren, whatsoever things are .

true, whatsoever things are honest, whatsoever things are just, whatsoever things are pure, whatsoever things are lovely, whatsoever things are of good report; if there be any virtue, and if there be any praise, think on these things" (Phil. 4:6-8). We have a Savior who loves us and gives us the answers to do all that He wants of us. Remember, right thinking leads to right living. Let us fill our minds and thoughts with truth. James, the half brother of our Lord writes: "But be ye doers of the word, and not hearers only...But whoso looketh into the perfect law of liberty, and continueth, he being not a forgetful hearer...This man shall be blessed in his deed" (James 1:22, 25).

Be Of Good Cheer. Those suffering with loneliness must take heart and "Be of Good Cheer." Jesus told many who were sick, despondent and unhappy to cheer up! The Master told this man sick of the palsy, lying on a bed, "Son, be of good cheer; thy sins be forgiven thee" (Matt. 9:2). Jesus further told a woman with a malady for 12 years, "Daughter, be of good comfort; thy faith hath made thee whole" (Matt. 9:22). Imagine going to the hospital to visit someone lying sick and telling them to "Cheer up!" Yet, that's what Jesus told the sick! Most of the time when visiting the sick all you hear is the list of all the miseries, aches and pains they have. We must exude a positive attitude that lends itself to an upbeat visit. As a shut-in we do not need to hear all the latest misery and disasters that have occurred. Those confined and isolated want positive information that will leave them feeling better when the visit ends.

The disciples were terrified of a fierce storm and the figure walking toward them. Jesus said, "Be of good cheer; it is I; be not afraid" (Matt. 14:27). How consoling and strengthening were these words in a time of fear and anxiety. To his faithful apostle Paul, who came near death in a riot in Jerusalem, Jesus said "Be of good cheer, Paul: for as thou hast testified of me in Jerusalem, so must thou bear witness also at Rome" (Acts 23:11). The Savior urged us to cheer up! In full view of life's many crises, Jesus encouraged us with this word of reassurance: "Be of good cheer, I have overcome the world" (Jn. 16:33). If we are to be full of cheer in sickness, terror and turmoil, how much more should we be cheerful in the good times of sunshine and plenty? Solomon writes, "A merry heart doeth good like a medicine: but a broken spirit drieth the bones" (Prov. 17:22).

A *New York Times* article revealed the research of Dr. Daniel Mark, a heart specialist at Duke University. The *Times* article carried this headline: "Optimism Can Mean Life for Heart Patients and Pessimism Death." The article begins with these words: "A healthy outlook helps heal the heart." But another heart specialist, Dr. Nancy Frasure Smith, who has studied the effects of stress, anxiety, and anger, admitted, "We don't know how to change negative emotions." Those suffering loneliness and other negative emotions must see that faith in God can produce that change. We must put our trust in the Lord, "Trust in the Lord with all thine heart; and lean not unto thine own understanding" (Prov. 3:5).

Be Confident In The Hope Of God. God's faithful people see the bright side of life because they can look beyond this transitional world. The vision of the lonely person becomes shortsighted and limited, which causes short-term solutions. Abraham's faith and patience faced an important test while waiting for a son as he exceeded the years of fathering a child. Abraham, the father of many nations, was 100 years old when the birth of Isaac occurred (Gen. 21:1-8). Abraham against hope believed in hope, that he might become the father of many nations, according to God's will (Gen. 17:4-5). Abraham staggered not at the promise of God through unbelief; but was strong in faith, giving glory to God (Rom. 4:20). Abraham fully persuaded in what God promised, wavered not in faith knowing that He was able to perform (Rom. 4:21). He was optimistic because by his hope he could see the unseen.

The three Hebrew children faced the fiery furnace with optimism because of their hope in their Lord. "Shadrach, Meshach, and Abednego, answered and said to the king, O Nebuchadnezzar, we are not careful to answer thee in this matter. If it were so, our God whom we serve is able to deliver us from the burning fiery furnace, and he will deliver us out of thine hand, O king. But if not, be it known unto thee, O king, that we will not serve thy gods, nor worship the golden image which thou hast set up" (Dan. 3:16-18). Many

Old Testament characters had an unshakable faith, having hope in God, yet faced trouble and danger many times over. Regardless of the event or circumstance that brought us to the state of despair or loneliness, let us hang on and embrace the "hope of glory" (Col. 1:27). We are to face the future with confidence as hope brings gladness. "The hope of the righteous shall be gladness: but the expectation of the wicked shall perish" (Prov. 10:28).

Hope provides joy to the believer and gives cause for rejoicing. We should find satisfaction with the knowledge of living in a covenant relationship with God. Paul writes confidently, "For I know whom I have believed, and am persuaded that he is able to keep that which I have committed unto him against that day" (2 Tim. 1:12). Rejoicing in hope while exercising patience in great misfortune will bring us to fervent prayer (Rom. 12:12). The apostle writes, "Now the God of hope fill you with all joy and peace in believing, that ye may abound in hope, through the power of the Holy Spirit" (Rom. 15:13). Hope will undergird us with confidence. "But Christ as a son over his own house; whose house are we, if we holdfast the confidence and the rejoicing of the hope firm to the end" (Heb. 3:6).

May our readers fill their hearts with joy and hope as each person comes to grip with the problem of loneliness. God has not placed us here on this earth to absorb his sunshine and then radiate gloom. It is impossible to be faithful, hopeful, prayerful and pessimistic at the same time. There will be ups and downs in life and making these changes is essential. This author has come to realize that facing a permanent disability demands adjusting to an abnormal lifestyle. Many intersections appear on the road of life demanding change. These changes can be challenging, but also provides the potential for growth. If you are suffering loneliness, accept it as an opportunity to alter your life and reach another level in your spiritual development.

TOPICS FOR DISCUSSION

1. What is the definition of loneliness?

2. What are some the causes of loneliness?

3. Name some misconceptions of loneliness?

4. What are some practical ways that indicate loneliness?

5. Name four things that will help us to overcome loneliness?

Chapter Nine

When Parents Face Disorderly Children

9

Genesis 6:7 asserts: "But Noah found grace in the eyes of the Lord." This patriarch of the Old Testament lived in a time when the "wickedness of man was great in the earth, and that every imagination of the thoughts of his heart was evil continually" (Gen. 6:6). Just imagine the moral climate that existed as Noah and his wife raised their family, yet all signs suggest their children were submissive and obedient. The contemporaries of Noah were different as their bent toward sin was obvious. Consider this period of time when sin was widespread and menacing, as the hearts of men had become permeated with wickedness. Our 21st century is becoming more corrupt and raising a family more difficult than ever before. Pressures of the world can bring chaos on the family unit and will present challenges unimagined to those family members.

INTRODUCTION

This chapter is not an effort to blast adolescents, teenagers, or any other age group included in the family unit. Our purpose is to examine the state of the home, the responsibility of parents, the duty of children, and the pattern God has imposed on us to produce the home, as God would have it. God created man and woman in garden of Eden and there they remained until sin drove them out, banished from the tree of life (Gen. 3:23-24). Under indictment of sin Adam and Eve went forth from the garden and began to carve out a place for themselves, which we call a home.

During this time children became part of the family as Cain and Abel came from this union (Gen. 4:1-2). It did not take long before sin entered the heart of Cain and jealousy provoked him to slay his brother, Abel (Gen. 4:8).

God not only created the marriage union (Gen. 2:21-24), He also provided the needed arrangement and organization for a successful family unity (Eph. 5:22–6:4). The home in this century is under attack from many directions. We do not have to document for you the divorce rate that has been increasing over the last twenty-five years or so. There has been enough evidence, which shows the splintering of the home and the linkage to divorced parents. More than 50 percent of children born in the U.S. come outside the marriage union. Far too many children are brought up without the make-up of a mother and father in the home. It has also surfaced that more than half the couples in our country do so without the benefit of marriage. Those who cohabitate together in the presence of children are absent of real commitment, moving from one mate to another and subjecting their children to such unstable and changing environments (Heb. 12:6-8). This ungodly and unbridled lust has created an amoral climate for children preventing them from having a home life as God ordains (Rom. 7:1-3; 1 Cor. 7:2-4). Cohabitation on a high scale will weaken any society and will eventually cause its downfall.

STATE OF THE HOME

There was a recent report (October of 2002) by researchers at Child Trends, a national teen survey that has been tracking about 8,000 teens since 1997. The ages of the teens ranged from 12-16 when the survey began, and researchers interviewed the same group every year since then. This survey revealed that 34 percent of ninth graders had experienced sexual relations. The survey revealed that 60 percent of this group reaching their senior year was sexually active. Unfortunately 26 percent converted to this unchaste conduct during this intervening period.

Notice the following research Data:
• 56 percent experienced sex at their home or at the home of their partner
• 42 percent said their first sexual experience was between 10 p.m. and 7 a.m.
• 28 percent further said it was in the evening, between 6-10 p.m.

- 15 percent said it was in the late afternoon, between 3-6 p.m.
- 12 percent had their first sexual experience at a friend's house.
- 9 percent at a teen's own home
- 4 percent in a truck or car
- 3 percent at a park or other outdoor place
- 3 percent at a hotel or motel

Reading this recent survey of teenagers and their sexual conduct is deplorable and disturbing. Note some of the causes that may have contributed to this problem: A lack of parental influence and discipline, peer pressure, compromising one's moral principles, or surrendering to the unbridled appetites of the flesh. The apostle Paul writes the youthful Timothy, "Let no man despise thy youth; but be thou an example of the believers, in word, in conversation, in charity, in spirit, in faith, in purity" (1 Tim. 4:12). This holy admonition is just as current to our modern youth as the day Paul wrote them. **Abstinence from sex until marriage** is not only relevant, but all teens should give this way of life serious thought in a loose and lax society. The best gift that we can bring to the marriage alter is the purity of our morals. God designed sexuality for husband and wife. Expressing ourselves sexually is to be a wholesome, nurturing, and expressive way to show love to our marriage partner.

Interesting Facts About Alcohol–Alcohol has always contributed to suffering and heartache in the home. Below are some interesting facts about alcohol .

and the obvious impact it has on the home in our communities.

- Better than 50% of all teenagers drink alcohol in some form.
- One of every four teenage drinkers is a problem drinker or alcoholic.
- Almost 50,000 people die each year in traffic accidents, more than half are alcohol related–about 28,000.
- 2 of every 3 murders committed in this nation occur when the perpetrator has at least a 0.10% blood alcohol level.
- The suicide rate for alcoholics is 58% greater than for non-drinkers.
- Alcoholics are 7 times more likely to divorce or separate in their marriage.
- The children of alcoholics are twice as likely to become alcoholics as the children of non-alcoholics.
- Sixty percent of all child abuse cases involve alcohol.

The statistical information above highlights the moral decay of the home in America. May we consider the sanctity of the home and honor it to the station it richly deserves. One of the great leaders of our nation stated, "The home is the bedrock of our nation."

RESPONSIBILITY·OF PARENTS

The word "Parent" comes from a Latin word that means, "bring forth" or "beget." It originally described the power or gift of husbands and wives through the biological procedure to give birth to children. Hundreds of families from various states in the U.S. have expressed to me the realization that two people having the physical ability to "bring forth" children do not make them parents. To increase or multiply our own kind is a matter of biology; unfortunately we have all seen scores of couples who do not what parenting is all about.

David wrote the following: "Lo, children are an heritage of the Lord: and the fruit of the womb is his reward. As arrows are in the hand of a mighty man, so are children of the youth..." (Psm. 127:3-5). What has happened with parents today? Ann Landers, the famous columnist, reported that 70% of her readers said they would not have children if they could live their lives over. This is an alarming number and should stir us all to ponder the cause of such anxiety that now exists in our nation. It is this humble writer's opinion that a generation of parents have subscribed to the psychology of Dr. Benjamin Spock. His basic thesis presents the theory that children should not yield to corporeal punishment, as it will deform the psyche of the child. Such advise has led to a generation of children not receiving the discipline needed. The wise man said, "Foolishness is bound in the heart of a child; but the rod of correction will drive it far from him" (Prov. 22:15). This sage advise will go a long way toward correcting the problems of our children today.

There is nothing more important than knowing the destiny of a precious life, the life of a child, which depends on the role of a mother and father as directed by God. Summarizing the task under consideration comes in the words of Proverbs 22:6 "Train up a child in the way he should go, and even when he is old he will not depart from it." What does the word "train" mean? It means more than ordering or commanding. It is from the Hebrew word chanak–meaning "to put in one's mouth...To start, to lay the groundwork of character, to instill principles." It is all the influences that contribute to developing a child: telling, teaching, example, guidance, counseling, discipline, correction, restraint, and advice. The parents of the child are the primary standard in training the child.

1. Parents are the principle agents of this training. Parents largely have abandoned the control of children's minds to schools, the church, mass media, and classmates or friends. That parents are wringing their hands over this alarming trend is indisputable. What, then, does the Creator expect of husbands and wives who become fathers and mothers? He expects exactly what He approved in His faithful servant Abraham: "For I have known him to the end that he may command his children and his household after him, that they may keep the way of the Lord, to do righteousness and justice"(Gen. 18:19). In past days with everyone present in one place, someone might remark: "Well now, who is watching the store?" Today, we need to ask both the mother and father busily at work, "Just who is watching the kids?"

2. Parents are to begin early in training their children. When parents lose the early confrontations with the child, the later conflicts become harder to win. Parents who badly give up ground to the child, who are too tired or too busy to win, are making a costly mistake that will come back to haunt him during the child's adolescence.

If you can't make a five-year-old pick up his toys, it is unlikely that you will exercise any degree of control during his adolescence, the most defiant time of life. It is important to understand that adolescence is a composite of all the training and behavior that has gone before. Any unsettled matter in the first twelve years is likely to fester and bring serious discipline problems (Deut. 11:18-23).

3. Parents are to love their children with a fervent heart. Paul told Titus to "speak thou the things which befit the sound doctrine," which included teaching older women to "train the young women...to love their children"(Titus 2:3-4). Children needing affection from their parents is as basic as the nature of man himself. Children need love as infants, but also as adolescents and adults. Love in its purest form is offering attention: playing with the child, listening to him, answering his questions, helping him with homework, showing interest in his hobbies, and firmness for his mistakes. Love is saying to children by teaching and actions that they are no bother, that they are important and that mother and father love having them around.

4. Parents are to be good examples before their children. There cannot be a more powerful way, in .

the training formula, of guiding the lives of our children than setting the right example (Matt. 5:16). Jesus, for example, saw in His work the need to leave man "an example that ye should follow his steps" (1 Peter 2:21). Paul urged Christians to follow him as he mimicked Christ (1 Cor. 11:1).

Parents as examples call to mind several key biblical illustrations:

- The mother and grandmother of Timothy.
- Timothy was, of all of Paul's helpers, the most dedicated.
- Paul tells the Philippians that none of his co-workers was as unselfishly devoted to their needs as Timothy (Phil. 2:19-22).
- When writing to Timothy himself, Paul noted his sincere faith "which dwelled first in thy grand-mother Lois, and thy mother Eunice" (2 Tim. 1:5).
- Timothy as an evangelist walked by faith and cared spiritually for others, in part, because of what he viewed as a child in his mother and grandmother.

5. Parents are to nurture their children. Training children demands that parents, in the words of Paul, "nurture them in the chastening and admonition of the Lord" (Eph. 6:4). Remember, parents, the Lord did not give this responsibility to the church. The church has its assigned duty to teach and preach the gospel to every creature (Mark 16:15-16). However, what the church does in a limited way does not fulfill the duty God gave to parents (Eph. 6:1-4). The word "nurture" means "to nourish, promote health and strength." The term "chastening" shows "child training" and refers to rearing children. Teaching, correcting, disciplining, and loving are all included in this responsibility.

6. Parents are to discipline their children. Teaching children is not enough. What we teach must come enforced with discipline. Parents until recent years have known the value of saying "no" and punishing disobedient children. Believers in God have always known: "He that spareth the rod hateth his son; but he that loveth him chasteneth him betimes" (Prov. 13:24). The writer of Hebrews discusses discipline in describing God's familiarity to Christians (Heb. 12:5-11).

• He parallels God's role to the duty of parents.
• He says that God's discipline of His children comes out of love.
• Parents, therefore, must discipline their children because they care, and because a lesson to their welfare becomes essential.
• When discipline comes out of love it promotes reverence, respect, and subjection by the children.

RESPONSIBILITY OF CHILDREN

Consider the wise man's admonition to "Train up a child in the way he should go, and even when he is old he will not depart from it" (Prov. 22:6). Do children have a responsibility in their own training procedure?

• The method of training is not a one-way street, involving only parents! It is not complete until the child accepts the training.

• Suppose someone says this (object) is yours, unless you take it from me you will never have it despite my offer.

• God gives us His saving by grace, but until fully accepted with compliant obedience, salvation will never come to realization (Eph. 2:8-9; 1 Peter 1:22).

• A teacher teaches–the pupil learns. However, no learning takes place until something happens by the learner.

• Conversely, parents provide the teaching, guidance, correction, and love in the child, but he still has not reached the trained plateau until there is a positive response by the child.

The author is not trying to excuse or give comfort to careless parents who have shirked their duty. Our hope is to awaken parents and children both to the duties each has in the training approach. The supreme goal of training is to lead one to enjoy a right relationship with God.

TOPICS FOR DISCUSSION

1. What was the secret to Noah's success in raising their children?

2. What stunning statistics show the state of the home in America?

3. Name some of the major problems that our children face in our world.

4. Name one basic reason for parents failing in their duty as mother and father.

5. Do children have a role to play in the "training" formula? What is most important to you?

Chapter Ten

The
Modern Family
In Trouble

10

The oldest institution created of God is the home (Gen. 1-2). This divine institution had its origin in the Garden of Eden and from that place in paradise the home was a precious gem seen as essential to man's civilization. God is the author of the home and has sanctioned through His word to regulate, mold, and form the home. It is the ideal place to fulfill the physical, social, and emotional needs of men and women (Gen. 2:18-24). The home is also the perfect arrangement and environment for the upbringing and nurturing of children (Eph. 6:1-4). The problems we face in this land of liberty are many, yet at the root of our ills is the acute dysfunction of the home. A growing number of sociologists, psychologists, and others are telling us the traditional home in America is on the endangered species list. Most social ills facing our wonderful and once strong country stem from problems in the home and we must address them thoughtfully.

Many, however, are proud of the new modern family in America with its deviant lifestyle. The new family highlighted by those trying to restructure the biblical pattern of the home has attacked this divine institution leaving it a shell of what deity intended. The University of Chicago conducted a survey that reveals the percentage of American households made up of married couples with children. Surprisingly the number of couples living together as husband and wife dropped from 45 percent in the early 1970's to just 26 percent in the 1998 survey. This figure suggests a dramatic increase in couples that are now living together without the benefit of marriage. Fornication is like a runaway train, unbridled in our land and glorified daily on television and more so on the silver screen (1 Thess. 4:3-6). The home has been the object of scorn and ridicule by the Hollywood crowd with a clear motivation to promote same sex marriage, cohabitation, and other unnatural acts that will bring about the death of the home.

STATISTICS ALARMING

There are many troubles that persist in the America culture about the home. Slowly and subtly the progressive and intellectual crowd is telling us the traditional home in America is on the brink of extinction. Most social ills facing our wonderful and once strong country stem from problems in the homes across this nation.

The most recent government census (2000) reveals some interesting facts and figures to all that have the courage to read the signs and heed the warnings. The census reveals that unwed people living together jumped 71.7 percent during the 1990's. This is an astounding number and little wonder the family, as we know it, is the object of such contempt.

According to the census, single women raising children grew five times faster than married couples raising children. David Murray, director of Statistical Assessment Service, a Washington based think tank, said, "We are on the verge of a new experiment in American life. A significant portion of young people will not know the family comprised of a married father and mother."An article appearing in The Orlando Sentinel, May 15, 2001 stated, "The latest information shows the American family, like a boat without a rudder, in a continuing state without a compass, combined with an increased number of people living together outside marriage and more single women raising children." Some have found positive good about the findings of the census report, and it appears divorce is dropping off. What they fail to recognize is that marriage is on the decline, and that more people are just living together! Another alarming fact emanating from the census is: "The growing number of unmarried partners, which reached 5.5 million in 2000, also includes same-sex relations and older people living together, but those numbers won't be available until further census analysis is released" (Orlando Sentinel, May 15, and 18, 2001).

A timely article appeared in the **Denver Post** titled "Survey reveals major changes in U.S. family"

(November 24, 1999). It stated, "The single-earner families with young children still present in the household have become the exception rather than the rule." It further reported that children left alone at home often become identified as "latchkey" children. To think there are significantly fewer couples living by the guidelines of marriage than those cohabiting without the sanction of God's plan is disturbing.

The survey in 1998 discovered the percentage of children living with single parents rose to 18.2 percent, versus 4.7 percent in 1972. A family is to consist of husband and wife (Eph. 5:22). All of us realize that circumstances can justifiably alter the ideal, such as the death of a spouse. However, these statistics suggest something more serious: More and more women are electing to have children out of marriage contrary to the divine plan of God. More than a decade ago the Vice President of the U.S. gave a scathing speech ridiculing Hollywood and the television industry for portraying a fictitious character, Murphy Brown, for having a child without the benefit of marriage. The Vice President, ridiculed and mocked for his stand of promoting family values has become a champion for decency and having the courage to cry out on such an important subject. The moral clarity of this brave politician exposed the deviant lifestyle promoted by the purveyors of the entertainment Mecca of the world. Also, the numbers are on the decline who marry, and at the first sign of trouble the dissolution comes in a courtroom with the judge thrusting his gavel down, saying, "Divorce granted." We must have a revival of the marriage institution and respect those accepting the permanent vows–"until death do us part." The Savior's words ring from the Holy Scripture addressing the sanctity and permanence of marriage and could not ring with greater clarity (Matt. 5:32; 19:9).

The Denver Posts states, "Researchers at the University of Chicago said their findings suggest the face of the American family has changed." The article continues, "While June Cleaver might not approve, the American people are accepting the 'modern family' with all the departures and unconventional ways that abandon God's design of the home." How sad! (Prov. 13:15; Gal. 6:7-8).

WHAT GOD HATH JOINED TOGETHER

When one carefully considers God's word, clearly the heavenly Father has joined certain matters together. Further, truth and error like oil and water do not mix. Man must learn to distinguish between God's commands, and to learn the difference between context and the covenants. Nonetheless, man seems forever busy, even religious leaders, trying to divide and distort the straightforward commands binding on us today.

God joins husband and wife. God is the author of marriage and blesses the union of man and woman (Gen. 2:18-25; Heb. 13:4). Jesus reaffirmed God's original marriage statute, "And said, for this cause shall a man leave father and mother, and shall cleave to his wife: and they twain shall be one flesh?

Wherefore they are no more twain, but one flesh. What therefore God hath joined together, let not man put asunder" (Matt. 19:5-6). There is much debate among many that look for "a loophole" about divorce and remarriage. Jesus said, "Whosoever shall put away his wife, except it be for fornication, and shall marry another, committeth adultery: and whoso marrieth her which is put away doth commit adultery" (Matt. 19:9). God united man and woman together in marriage. Jesus shows that God's law never changed with death breaking this union (Rom. 7:2). However, the Nazarene gave one exception to the general rule of divorce and remarriage, fornication. Neither husband nor wife has the right to divorce and remarry without fornication taking place. Only the innocent party has the right to remarry while the guilty party does not. Man often "breaks the bond of marriage," by rejecting the heavenly Father's clear-cut command. Sadly, divorce and remarriage is raging in our nation and far too many are surrendering to this sin, which will come with certain retribution from the God of heaven. The prophet, Malachi, said, "For the Lord, the God of Israel, saith that He hateth the putting away (divorce)" (Mal. 2:16).

Blessings and faithfulness together. God has always combined blessings with our faithfulness. However, to hear those teach that man's conduct has nothing to do with submission to God's Word shows woefully ignorance and their charge is totally false. Undeniably, the scriptures connect our faithfulness with God's blessings. Please consider James' statement, .

"Blessed is the man that endureth temptation: for when he is tried, he shall receive the crown of life, which the Lord hath promised to them that love him" (James 1:12). Jesus said, "If ye know these things, blessed are ye if ye do them" (John 13:17, ASV).

PRESCRIPTION FOR TROUBLED HOMES

A man shall cleave to his wife. "Therefore shall a man leave his father and his mother, and shall cleave to his wife: and they shall be one flesh" (Gen. 2:24). Notice that this verse is teaching commitment and dedication, not just cohabitating together. Many Americans today refuse to accept commitment and responsibility. Marriage is urgently important and must come first, superceding the love of mother and father.

The husband is the head and viewed as the provider. The scriptures are plain in the fact of headship (Gen. 3:16; 1 Cor. 11:3; Eph. 5:22-24). The wife's submission to her husband's rule illustrates accepting the church to Jesus' headship (Eph. 5:22). The husband is to love (agapao, have her best interest in mind) his wife, as Christ loved the church and gave himself for her (Eph. 5:25). The wife is the "keeper of the home" (Titus 2:5; Prov. 31:10). The husband is the chief provider (Gen. 3:17-19; 1 Tim. 5:8; Prov. 31:10).

The wife is the glue and support of the family unit. The woman plays a significant role in the home. Titus encourages women, "To be discreet, chaste, keepers at home, obedient to their own husbands, that the word of God be not blasphemed" (Titus 2:5). God knew the woman would find her skills excelling in the domestic affairs of the home. This does not mean, of course, that she cannot go out and help her husband if such is necessary. Even the "worthy woman" in Proverbs 31:11-16 was an industrious businesswoman more than willing to help her family. The wife must not neglect her domestic duties, as busy as she might become, as her calling from God is clear and certain. Personal note: Husbands' should not think they are above helping their spouse in such domestic chores. A powerful statement from the inspired pen of Paul, "So ought men to love their wives as their own bodies. He that loveth his wife loveth himself" (Eph. 5:28).

Children must learn to honor and respect their parents. The scriptures teach, "Honor thy father and mother; which is the first commandment with promise; that it may be well with thee, and thou mayest live long on the earth" (Eph. 6:2-3). Parents should provide guidance and direction in the home while their children give respect and reverence to their parents, and not viewed as peers or pals. "Honor" suggests value, respect, and acts of kindness. It may also involve physical compensation if such becomes necessary when a parent needs support or help (Gen. 48:12; Prov. 3:9). Another growing problem in America is the aging population. Many expect the government to provide for this increasing segment of our society. However, God places the responsibility on children (see Matt. 15:4-6, 1 Tim. 5:4, 8).

The ideal family works in unison with God as their overseer. Relating the headship or make-up of the home, children are to be in subjection to their parents (Eph. 6:1-3). Parents must teach and provide spiritual training, discipline, and education for our children (Eph. 6: 4). Since God created man and established marriage and the family, it follows that the God of all creation receive honor and His laws be obeyed. Such is the ideal family. If our nation is to be turned around and rise out of the morass of loose morals and empty values, it must return to the Word of Truth (John 8:32; Psalms 119:89).

CONCLUSION

Beloved, since God is the author of the home, He knows our need for survival and success. It is not too late to restore the home, which is at the root of so many problems in society. It all begins with you and me as individuals. Let us make the home a place that our children will cherish when they grow older and can use as a model for their own homes. We have preached for many years that to reproduce the church of the New Testament is to follow the pattern God has given. The home as God would have it must follow the same model if this glorious institution will make a come back in an age of relativism and modernism.

TOPICS FOR DISCUSSION

1. What is the first divine institution created by God?

2. Why are there fewer marriages taking place today?

3. Why do you think the juvenile crime rate has increased so fast?

4. What is the single cause that undermines our homes today?

5. The prescription for troubled homes includes what?

Chapter Eleven

When Facing
Financial
Troubles

11

The Bible contains much information about the use and mishandling of our money, which is a serious issue to God. Considering God's obvious focus on money, shouldn't we–His children–be just as focused? This subject shall occupy our attention in this chapter. Biblical students have realized that a surplus of information exists on the subject of money or its misuse more than faith, repentance, confession, and baptism all put together. This subject should give us pause as we continue our pilgrimage on this earth.

Paul the apostle said: "He which soweth sparingly shall reap also sparingly; and he which soweth bountifully shall reap also bountifully. Every man according as he purposeth in his heart; so let him give; not grudgingly, or of necessity; for God loveth a cheerful giver" (2 Cor. 9:6-7). These verses open a minefield of interpretations, excuses and "it means something else" (whatever the something else might be at any given time). These verses in Holy Scripture have application to money. They also can apply to our commitment in support of the local preacher and the church.

They mean more than that, much more. God loves a cheerful giver, but had rather we refuse to give than to give grudgingly. Our response in giving back to the Creator must stem from a cheerful and grateful heart, or decline giving at all. He also tells us that we will only reap what we sow. We do not necessarily receive in kind the same blessings we gave, nor at the same time. We should give as we have prospered, and in like manner we will receive the blessings from God when needed and at His time.

BIBLE TRUTHS ABOUT: MONEY

A. Money Myths

1. **God's concern about money.** The Bible contains over 700 direct references about money, including 2/3 of the parables, and one out of every six verses in the Gospels concerns itself with the right and wrong use of material possessions.

2. **Money Matters are not Spiritual Matters.** Jesus tied our ability to handle spiritual blessings with our skill to handle money:

> If therefore ye have not been faithful in the unrighteous mammon (money), who will commit to your trust the true riches (Luke 16:11)?

The principle expressed in the Scriptures is the love of money is "a root of all kinds of evil..." (1 Tim.

6:9,10); not money itself. Money, in and of itself, is neither virtuous nor evil.

B. Money Truths
1. God owns you!

Yours, O LORD, is the greatness, the power and the glory, the victory and the majesty; for all that is in heaven and in earth is Yours. Yours is the kingdom, O LORD, and You are exalted as head over all (1 Chron. 29:11).

You are not your own; you were bought with a price... (1 Cor. 6:19-20).

2. We are to honor God with the first fruits of our increase–"When we give our tithes and offerings, we acknowledge our trust and faith in God as our provider and Lord" (See Prov. 3:9; Rom. 11:16). God loves and blesses generous givers (Prov. 11:25; 22:9; 2 Cor. 9:7). You can't out bless God! The blessings received are greater than the aptitude to give (Malachi 3:10; Acts 20:35).

3. **We are responsible to be good stewards with what God gives us.** "Moreover it is required in stewards that one be found faithful" (1 Cor. 4:2).

4. **God is our only provider.** "And my God shall supply all your need according to His riches in glory in Christ Jesus" (Phil. 4:19; See also Matt. 6:25-34). When we live a lifestyle of indebtedness, we are saying to the world, "God cannot take care of my needs–I must complement my income with other people's money." Indebtedness is also a sign of not trusting in God's provision (Matt. 6:30-32).

5. **The borrower is a slave to the lender.** "The rich rules over the poor, and the borrower is servant to the lender" (Prov. 22:7). So, when you borrow money, you place yourself in servitude to the one you borrow from!

6. **We are to owe to no one anything, except love!** "Owe no one anything except to love one another, for he who loves another has fulfilled the law" (Rom. 13:87).

7. **To follow God's ways, lend to many and borrow from none.** "You shall lend to many nations, but you shall not borrow" (Deut. 28:12). When the United States of America stopped following God's ways, it went from the biggest lender nation to the biggest borrower nation!

8. **Only God gives power to create true wealth.** Then you say in your heart, "My power and the might of my hand have gained me this wealth." And you shall remember the LORD your God, for it is He who gives you power to get wealth" (Deut. 8:17-18). Wealth comes from the Hebrew word 'CHAYIL' meaning strength, riches, plenty, and efficiency.

9. **When you borrow money, you are promising future income that does not belong to you!** "Do not boast about tomorrow, for you do not know what a day may bring forth" (Prov. 27:1).

10. **God showed His people to give to their own, without interest, or usury.** "To your brother you shall not charge interest, that the LORD your God may bless you in all to which you set your hand in the land which you are entering to possess" (Deut. 23:20).

THE TRUTH ABOUT OUR FINANCES

Facts about you and your money

- The average American will SPEND $1,860,000 on goods and services in his or her lifetime. (**American Demographics**)

- A baby boomer who makes $50,000 a year today will need ONE MILLION DOLLARS in savings to replace that income when retirement comes. (**USA Today**)

- The average cost of owning and keeping a car over the course of a person's working life will reach more than $200,000. (**American Institute for Economic Research**)

- If the cost of owning a car was cut in half (that is each car kept twice as long before replacement), **the savings invested at 10% over the same person's working life would build up to another $1,317,495 in retirement income!**

- An extra payment each month of $100 applied to a 9%, 30-year fixed $100,000 mortgage will save $75,394 in interest.

- Adding just 15% to your monthly mortgage payment can cut 10 to 15 years off the average mortgage.

- More than HALF of all the money you make in your lifetime will go towards taxes, debt payments, and fees.

- Average homeowners stay in their homes for 7.1 years (**National Association of Realtors®**). With an average 8% mortgage, they will sell their homes still owing over 90% of the principle. **If they continue**

this trend, they will NEVER pay off a home in their lifetimes!

- The average 45 to 54-year old has just $2,600 in the bank (**Capital Research Associates**)
- The average savings of a retired couple is only $7,000.
- "On average, Americans can expect to receive just 37% of the annual retirement income they will need to live comfortably" (**Oppenheimer Funds Dist., Inc.**)
- 85% of Americans have a true net worth of less than $250. (**Social Security Administration**)
- Every day, over 2,200 Americans lose their jobs.
- Parents can expect to pay over $150,000 to raise a child to age 18; and if the child goes to college, add another $70,000 to $160,000.

Unprecedented numbers of Americans are in debt for record amounts.

- 50 million credit cards come to citizens each year.
- 70% of those holding credit cards have a balance, which averages over $3,000.
- Payments on debt now account for 92% of family disposable income.
- Total consumer debt is over 5 trillion dollars. That's about the same as the government's "national" debt everyone keeps talking about.
- Personal bankruptcies are at an all-time high of about a million a year.

Banks, finance, and credit card companies have encouraged indebtedness

• Credit card companies are marketing to college students, so the borrowing habit begins in the earliest stages of adulthood.

• Credit cards used for groceries and rent are common today.

• Credit card companies offer low interest rates to entice borrowers to transfer balances from other cards. However, the rates then increase dramatically, usually after only six months.

• Many companies, like GE Capital Services, are now charging penalty fees to customers who **do not** carry a balance on their credit card.

• Credit card companies normally want minimum payments of only 3% of the outstanding balance. **But that means the typical $3,900 balance, at 18% interest, would take nearly 42 years to pay off, and those monthly payments would total $14,530.44.** Capital One advertises they'll lower your minimum payment from 3% to 2% for a fee. **What they don't tell you is that paying only 2% of your outstanding balance each month could make the bill last longer than you do.**

• People commonly borrow against their home equity. United Jersey Bank advertises minimum payments only on the interest, for up to ten years. **Imagine, ten years could pass, you could pay thousands of dollars, and still have made NO progress on reducing your loan.**

• Bank One is planning to test Visa and

MasterCard accounts that will allow you to borrow up to 40% of your 401K plan before retirement. Nothing like throwing away your future for a little immediate comfort.

Did you know?

• Every dollar you pay above the minimum monthly payment on a debt earns you **a gain equivalent to the interest rate the debt charges**. In other words, if you pay and extra $100 towards the balance of a credit card that charges 15% interest, you're getting the wealth building effect of earning 15% each year on that $100. That way is better than most investments over a period time. So the more you prepay against **debt** balances (without adding to them at the same time) the more you earn in effective interest.

• Prepaying your mortgage balance earns you more than you could possibly lose, **with the mortgage interest deduction**. Let's say you're in the 28% tax bracket. That means the government gives you a 28-cent tax break for every dollar you spend on mortgage interest. **But that means you're LOSING 72 cents out of each of those dollars.** If anyone tells you that paying a dollar to get back 28 cents is a good investment, suggest they should recheck their math.

What can you do?

. Begin erasing your debts with all speed.

. Never fall into the habit of making only minimum payments.

. Avoid the trap of thinking in monthly payments.

Consider the cost of buying the goods or service needed, not just whether you can fit the payment into your monthly budget. **Always think about how much the monthly payment could build up to over a couple decades if it was going into your retirement account instead of the credit company's profit account.**

DEFINITION OF "DEBT"

The word 'opheile' (of-i-lay) means, "That which is owed." Many "conventional" experts define debt as, "money borrowed on an item of depreciating value, thus implying that borrowing money on appreciating items is not debt. This is simply not brought out in the Biblical definition! Paul writes: "Owe no man anything, but to love one another" (Rom. 13:8). Paul is affirming that no debt should remain outstanding, except the continuing debt to love one another, for he who loves his fellowman has fulfilled the law. The demands of being debt free compels us to live according to Romans 13:8.

DEFINITION OF "PROSPEROUS LIVING"

1. **A form of the word "prosper" appears over 80 times in the Old and New Testaments.** The most common Hebrew word for "prosper" is *tsalach* (tsaw-lakh') it means, "to advance, make progress, succeed, be profitable. To bring to successful issue; to experience prosperity."

2. **Prosperity is a blessing from the Lord when people follow his ways.**

> Blessed is the man who walketh not in the counsel of the ungodly or standeth in the way of sinners, or sitteth in the seat of the scornful. But his delight is in the law of the Lord...And whatsoever he doeth shall prosper (Psm. 1:1-3).

> This Book of the Law shall not depart out of thy mouth; meditate therein day and night, that thou mayest observe to do according to all that is written therein. Then thou shalt make thy way and then thou shalt have good success (Josh. 1:8).

Solomon adds, "The blessing of the Lord brings wealth, and He addeth no sorrow to it" (Prov. 10:22). The Wiseman further states,

> Riches and honor are with me; yea durable riches and righteousness. My fruit is better than gold, yea, than fine gold and my revenue than choice silver. I lead in the way of righteousness...That I may cause those that love me to inherit substance and I will fill their treasures (Prov. 8:18-19, 21).

3. **Prosperity does not mean only financial riches**. This would be a narrow view of such a proposition. It simply means that we are living according to God's principles and enjoying His blessings. Further, journeying through our pilgrimage here on earth **free from greed, worry, and bondage** is a true blessing. "Beloved, I pray that you may prosper in all things and be in health, just as your soul prospers" (3 John 1:3). The Greek word "prosper" is

euodoo (yoo-od-o'-o), which means, "to have a successful journey through life." The Hebrew word *shalom* (shaw-lome') translated "prosperous" also means "Completeness, safety, health, soundness, and contentment" (Zech. 8:12).

4. **God is not against material riches as long as you recognize the Source and honor Him with your riches.** Paul writes, "That they do good, that they be rich in good works, ready to deal out, willing to communicate" (1 Tim. 6:17-19). The rich man in Luke 12, arrogant in his success, decides to build more barns while denying the source of his blessings. God said to him, "Thou fool, this night thy soul shall be required of thee; then whose shall those things be?" (Luke 12:20). Let us all remember that God is the origin of all material blessings and we are simple stewards.

5. **The Holy Scriptures teaches how we are to live within our means.** "But godliness with *contentment* is great gain" (1 Tim. 6:6) (emphasis added). Another Hebrew word for "prosper" is *sakal* (saw-kal') [same word for "success"] which means "to be prudent, to consider, be circumspect." In other words, to be cautious and good stewards of what God gives us (see 1 Kings 2:3 and "success" in Joshua 1:8).

6. **True prosperity hangs in the balance between being "rich" and being "poor."**

> Give me neither poverty nor riches, but give me only my daily bread. Otherwise I may have too much and disown you and say 'Who is the Lord?' Or I may become poor and steal and so dishonor the name of my God (Prov 30:8-9).

Biblically speaking, our heart can be wrong either with money–or **without** money–either by being greedy–or by worrying.

So we define Prosperous Living as... A way to stay free from debt slavery is to owe no one **anything** except to love. As far as your financial considerations, have a successful journey through life–to walk circumspectly and prudently–and be good stewards of what God gives you (1 Pet. 4:10).

CONCLUSION

Christians should be free to serve God and give generously to the kingdom of God and for its purposes (see 2 Cor 9:6-13; Prov 11:24-25).

We must learn to live within our means, be good stewards, and be content with what God gives us. We must show thanksgiving "occupied with gladness of heart" (see Eccl. 5:18-20). May God bless you in your service to follow God in all His ways!

TOPICS FOR DISCUSSION

1. What is the difference in giving cheerfully versus grudgingly?

2. How often is the use or misuse of our material blessings mentioned in Bible?

3. As stewards of our blessings, how severe will God exercise judgment?

4. Why is it important for Christians to learn about debt and financial responsibility?

5. Discuss the financial strain in the homes of America and the role it plays in the divorce rate?

Chapter Twelve

When Jacing Addictions

12

The apostle Paul writes to the Corinthians highlighting the glorious prize, the incorruptible crown, of the believers (1 Cor. 9:24-27). Paul compares himself to the racers and combatants in the games, and easily recognized by the Corinthians. Paul excites them to duty: "So run, that ye may obtain" (1 Cor. 9:24). Further, one cannot win the race unless prepared for the event. Paul directs the Corinthians, by setting himself as an example, as he sets forth the figure of a race. Those that ran in the games lived by a strict diet. All successful athletes realize that diet and discipline are important to their success. They do not indulge themselves, but feel compelled in their diligence and preparation. Those reaching for the crown were not only temperate, but also trained with enthusiasm to reach their goal. In the Christian race we must fight against our enemies with all our might. One enemy the apostle mentions is the body, which is under control as the combatants were in the Grecian games. The appetites of the flesh and needless wants wear against our bodies and thus our souls. The reward is an incorruptible crown, a crown that fadeth not away (James 1:12; 1 Peter 1:4).

Man in general and Christians in particular should follow the example of Paul, as he was "temperate in all things" (1 Cor. 9:25). This has application to our subject of addictions. The word temperate "engkrateuetai" means the exercise of "wrestling, boxing," or pitching a weight. It shows "self-restraint" from all that would excite, stimulate, and lastly weaken: from wine, from exciting and comfortable living, and from corrupt indulgences. It means that they did all they could to make the body vigorous, active, and resilient. Their aim was in pursuit of a course that leads to temperate living (compare Acts 24:25; 1 Cor. 7:9; Galatians 5:23; 2 Peter 1:6) **(Barnes' Notes, Electronic Database. Copyright (c) 1997 by Biblesoft).**

Living a "temperate" life is the total sum of our objective as Christians. The Bible (ASV) translates "temperate" as *self-control*, having the gift to control all features of our life. Those surrendering to addictions, regardless of what they may be, are intemperate and unable to control their lives. Paul affirms, "For ye are bought with a price: glorify God in your body, and in your spirit, which are God's" (1 Cor. 6:20). Those given over to addictions admit defeat, as they become a slave to their master. Jesus is our Savior and Master to whom we should give our loyalty and commitment. Anything that interferes with our devotion to Christ makes us a servant to it.

THESE ARE SOME OF THE CHARACTERISTICS OF AN ADDICT:

- They lack understanding toward others.
- They have a narrow range of emotions (usually limited to anger and elation).
- They likely will communicate on a shallow level finding it difficult to discuss their feelings.
- They live in a constant state of denial.
- They are unwilling to accept responsibility for their behavior and recovery.
- They project their own inadequacies on others and blame others for their problems.
- They are unable to keep promises or commitments.
- They are scheming and manipulative.
- Though abnormal, their addiction is their method of coping with life's stresses.

WE CANNOT OVERSTATE THE ADDICTION PROBLEM!

It consumes the addict's mind, body and soul as well as those who care for them. An addict's path of destruction will often impact the family, friends and co-workers and can be passed down to generations. Even though an addict may regret his or her behavior or the distress it causes family members, the addict remains powerless to the effects of their addiction.

MANAGING ADDICTIONS ALONE IS UNREALISTIC

It needs the support and cooperation of a

network of supporters. Conquering an addiction involves more than abstaining from the addictive behavior or acts because it involves examining and changing all the associated feelings and behaviors attached to the addiction. Therefore, the challenge of altering an addict's behavior and eventually helping him or her to overcome their addiction becomes doubly hard because to do so, the behavior of the codependent also needs to change. If you can identify with any of these "flags"...then you might want to ponder the possibility of being "an addict."

NOTE THE FOLLOWING ADDICTIONS

1. **Sexual Addiction**. The sexual revolution has made a permanent imprint on American life over the last thirty to forty years. Its impact has been subtle and minor in some ways while more pronounced in others. Movies and television began exploiting the sanctity and holiness of the sexual bond and now has promoted a loose life style that has permeated every portion of our culture. The television media has incrementally lowered the morals with programs coming into American homes, with subtle messages that would desensitize the viewers thinking on this and other moral issues.

The University of California at Santa Barbara conducted a survey that represents the most comprehensive findings yet on television's sexual messages. More than 1,351 references came from television shows, more than half of all programming, 56 percent excluding newscasts and children's shows, features sexual references or behavior. Primetime programming saw 67 percent, or two out of three programs, addressing sexual content. Soap operas, 85 percent of which contain sexual content, movies 83 percent and talk shows 78 percent focus on sex more consistently than any other subject.

SEXUAL ADDICTION STATISTICS

• Average age for first time contact with pornography is around 11 years old.

• Average age for seeking help is between 30-35.

• 80% of all married sex addicts thought marriage was the answer to their addiction.

• 50% of all alcoholics are sex addicts.

• 81% of all sex addicts became sexually abused themselves.

• 80% of spouses of sex addicts became sexually violated.

The church, neighborhood, school, or workplace is not immune to the devastating effects of pornography and the open sexual exploits, which gains ground with each passing day. Interviews of countless wives and husbands of sexual addicts has shown the destructive effects of both pornography and other sexual addictions. The Bible is clear in its condemnation of immoral sexuality and obsessive behavior. Peter describes the false teachers of his day, "Having eyes full of adultery, and that cannot cease from sin" (2 Peter 2:14). Those living in this kind of abnormal climate may overcome such through the blood of Christ. Paul tackles such behavior at Corinth by stating, "And such were some of you: but ye are washed, but ye are sanctified, but ye are justified in the name of the Lord Jesus..." (1 Cor. 6:11).

2. **Alcohol Addiction.** Surely no one can disagree that drug abuse is a serious problem among which alcohol heads the list. Like our English word, the Greek word for "drunk" refers to "intoxication, drunkenness...to get drunk, become intoxicated..." (Thayer). Romans 13:12-14 stresses that Christians must cast off the works of darkness and walk properly, not in drunkenness. Paul underlined that Christians should resist the effort to satisfy the lusts of the flesh. People who are guilty of drunkenness will not inherit the kingdom of God (Gal. 5:19-21; 1 Cor. 6:9-11). If a church member commits drunkenness and refuses to repent, discipline should come to bear and fellowship be withdrawn. So, whether caused by alcohol or by other drugs, intoxication violates God's word. But the use of any drug we are studying, including just one marijuana cigarette, causes intoxication (1 Cor. 5:11).

ALARMING ALCOHOL STATISTICS

- Alcohol is a 40 billion dollar a year business in the US.
- Better than 50% of all teenagers drink alcohol in some form.
- One of every four teens becomes a problem drinker or alcoholic.
- More than five percent of America's workforce is alcoholic.
- Of about 50,000 lives lost each year in traffic

accidents, more than half are alcohol related–about 28,000.

• For every dollar raised in tax revenue in this country, more than four dollars become lost in alcohol-related expenses. Such problems as lost production, health and medical care, motor vehicle accidents, violent crimes, and fire loses.

• 2 of every 3 murders committed occurs when the perpetrator has at least a 0.10% blood alcohol level.

• The suicide rate for alcoholics is 58% greater than for non-drinkers.

• Alcoholics are 7 times more likely to become divorced or separated.

• The children of alcoholics are twice as likely to become alcoholics as the children of non-alcoholics.

• Sixty percent of all child neglect cases involve alcohol.

• Alcohol is the #1 cause of preventable birth defects. Social drinking is one of the methods used to justify consuming alcohol.

Surveys report that 1 out of every 12 social drinkers become addicted. Studies have shown that moderate social drinking destroys brain cells. Prof. Melvin Knisely, of South Carolina University, has stated: "When the drinkers begins to feel light-headed or giddy, brain cells become destroyed." Paul writes, "All things are lawful unto me, but all things are not expedient: all things are lawful for me, but I will not be brought under the power of any" (1 Cor. 6:12). With these words Paul condemns social drinking. Alcohol is a drug and brings one under its power.

Alcoholics drink beer, ale and wine, among other drinks, and consume "ethyl alcohol," which is a habit-forming narcotic drug. Alcohol is a menace to our homes with a quarter of all divorces related to alcohol. Alcohol is a menace to business with 20 percent of all industry absenteeism because of alcohol and wage losses amount to more than four hundred fifty million dollars annually. It would be redundant to say that alcohol is a menace to our economy with more than 50 billion dollars lost annually through accidents, illness and sick leave involving drinking employees. This addiction is a chief concern to us and a threat to our soul salvation.

3. **Drug Addiction.** Many forces influence people, especially young people, to begin drug use. Modern music, movies, and TV programs glorify illegal drugs, such as marijuana. "Today, marijuana use has become promoted and used at concerts, on CDs, even on clothes–sending teens a message of social acceptance." Many of the specific examples cited come from **USA Weekend**, 2/16-18/1996.

Drug users time and again surround young people at school. I once asked a group of public school junior high and high school students, who attend the Lord's church, how many personally knew people who used drugs. Seven out of eight said they did. School drug programs offer to help solve the problem. But nearly all of them teach situation ethics. This subtle and crafty doctrine would leave it up to each person whether to use drugs in moderation, or if acceptable as long as you do not become intoxicated. They do not teach kids to avoid drugs, not even illegal drugs! Our purpose is to examine the problem of drug abuse in the backdrop of Bible teaching. We are not considering drugs prescribed by a doctor for medical purposes (1 Tim. 5:23). We are discussing mind-altering drugs used for social purposes (partying, peer pressure), or to escape reality, or just to enjoy the effect on the mind. We pray that our readers will consider carefully the information with an open mind and heart.

MARIJUANA USE IN AMERICA

In the 1970s, the baby boom generation was coming-of-age, and its drug of choice was marijuana.

• By 1979, more than 60 percent of 12th graders had tried marijuana at least once.

• 12th graders who had ever used marijuana decreased for more than a decade, dropping to a low of 33 percent in 1992.

• However, in 1993, first-time marijuana use by 12th graders was on the upswing, reaching 50 percent by 1997.

• In 1999, more than 2 million Americans used marijuana for the first time. Two-thirds of them were between the ages of 12 and 17.

Further, the marijuana today can be 5 times more potent than the marijuana of the 1970's. The use of marijuana can produce harmful physical, mental, emotional, and behavioral changes, and--contrary to popular belief--it can be addictive. Marijuana smoke, like cigarette smoke, can harm the lungs. The use of marijuana can damage short-term memory, verbal skills, and distort awareness. It also may weaken the immune organism and possibly increase a user's likelihood of developing cancer. Finally, the increasing use of marijuana by young teenagers may have an intensely negative effect on their development.

We hope that this material will help make readers aware of the current knowledge of marijuana abuse and it's harmful effects. (Glen R. Hanson, Ph.D., D.D.S.– **National Institute on Drug Abuse**).

STIMULANTS

These stimulate the nervous system, including the brain. This mainly includes amphetamines ("speed," "uppers," "dexies," and "bennies"). Some people classify cocaine here, but others view it as a narcotic. Short-term effects (immediate effects under the influence of the drug): Blurred vision, sleeplessness, stress, moodiness, and a high (intoxication) with a false sense of self-confidence, power, and well-being. Can produce hallucinations (seeing or hearing things that are not present), delusions (irrational thought), paranoia (thinking people are out to get you), or violent behavior. Overdoses can cause death.

SEDATIVES OR HYPNOTICS

Opposite to stimulants, these depress the nervous system, including the brain. Includes barbiturates ("barbs," "downers"). Heroine, other opiates, and marijuana become identified here. Short-term effects such as intoxication causes slurred speech, staggering, poor judgment and reflexes. Large doses can cause unconsciousness or death. Addicts may become so confused that he will take more drugs without realizing the outcome. Addiction is common. Users think they must have the drug to work. Getting drugs becomes the main role of life. Tolerance calls for a greater amount of drugs to get the same effect, while stopping causes extreme withdrawal effects (can be worse than heroin withdrawal): anxiety, convulsions, even death.

HALLUCINOGENS (PSYCHEDELICS)

These affect the brain causing one to lose touch with reality, seeing and hearing that which is not present (hallucinations). Includes LSD, mescaline, and PCP. Short-term effects: Effects are unpredictable. Rapid mood swings, loss of sense of reality, seeing and hearing the unreal; panic, confusion, anxiety. Bizarre, violent, and dangerous behavior can result (such as thinking one can fly, so he jumps off a tall building). Art Linkletter's daughter jumped to her death in this fashion. LSD can cause flashbacks in which the effects can repeat themselves days or weeks after taken. Possible brain damage, damaged memory, mental confusion. Dangerous acts while under the influence can lead to injury or death.

NARCOTICS

This includes derivatives of the opium plant: opium, morphine, codeine, and heroin. Narcotics may have a positive use medically and used as pain killers.

Some authorities include cocaine in this category. Short-term effects: In a state of being "high" or intoxicated, with a false sense of well-being. May alternate between drowsiness and alertness. Large doses can cause death. Addiction is almost certain. Finding the drug becomes the main focus of life, as tolerance needs larger doses to get the same effect. Eventually the user needs the drug just to work and avoid withdrawal.

DRUG ABUSE IS ILLEGAL

All of these drugs are illegal without a doctor's prescription. Most, if not all, cannot buy the drugs without a prescription. The drugs are used for social purposes, personal pleasure, to get a high and to escape reality is illegal. Specifically, marijuana is illegal to sell, give away, or even own. Possession of less than an ounce might lead to a year in prison, and possession of over an ounce can lead to several years in prison (according to Fort Wayne, Indiana, police department).

To disobey civil law is to sin against God. Romans 13:1-5–God ordained governing authorities. To resist them is to resist God's ordinance. The authorities may punish those who disobey, but they also have seared their conscience toward God (1 Peter 2:13-14). We must agree to every ordinance of man for the Lord's sake (Titus 3:1). This ought to settle the matter for every true believer. Drug abuse, including marijuana use, is illegal and therefore sinful. Some people favor legalization of marijuana. But even if ·

legalized, there are reasons why Christians should not use it.

People need to realize that Jesus, not drugs, is the answer to their need. God provides the means to handle any temptation or problem in life. You do not need to escape reality with drugs. You can avoid drugs and find your needs met in Jesus (1 Cor. 10:13). Paul writes the comforting words, "I can do all things through Christ which strengthenth me" (Phil. 4:13). All needed blessings will come by Jesus, which provides life and godliness (2 Peter 1:3). A life of drugs is a life of anguish, hopelessness, guilt, sorrow, and eventual death physically and eternally. Jesus is the real answer. His way is a way of life, hope, salvation, forgiveness, and eternal life (Psa. 138:3; Rom. 8:31-39; James 1:17; Eph. 3:20-21; 5:18).

4. **Gambling Addiction**. Why is there so much silence in pulpits and Bible classes about gambling? When did you last hear a lesson taught on the evils of gambling? Satan has lulled us to sleep about this dreaded sin as our society has become passionate to the mirage of a quick fix through gambling.

Definition of gambling–"gambling" refers to a wager or bet in which each player agrees to risk losing some material possession to other players. This game of chance will succeed in exchange for a chance to win the possessions of other players without compensation to the loser. The winner and loser will come to a resolution by the outcome of the game.

1. **A game of chance or skill - any event of uncertain outcome.** This may be a game the gamblers

play among themselves or may be some event that would have occurred anyway (such as the outcome of an election or sports event).

2. **The stakes.** Each player places at risk some possession of material value.

3. **The agreement (wager or bet).** Before the game each player *agrees* to risk losing his possession in exchange for the opportunity to take the possessions of others, depending on the outcome of the game.

4. **Lack of fair compensation.** No goods or services of fair value will come in exchange for that which becomes lost. The loser will give up his possessions without payment, and the winner will gain possessions without repaying the loser.

ACTIVITIES THAT ARE NOT GAMBLING

People sometimes confuse the issue by claiming that certain acts are gambling, even though some essential basics are missing.

Crossing the street, driving a car. Some people say, "Everything in life involves a gamble." This confuses risk with gambling. Not all risks involve gambling. These acts involve no wager and no stakes. There is no agreement to try to take someone else's possessions.

Farming, owning a business, etc. Some say this is gambling because one risks losing money. But again there is no wager, but there is compensation. There is no agreement to take other people's property without compensation. The intent is to produce goods or services of benefit to others in exchange for that which benefits us. The Scripture does not forbid farming and/or business.

Investing in stock. Some say this is gambling, but what is stock? Stock is a means for people to become part owners of a company. Buying stock is no more inherently gambling than is ownership of any other business. The intent is to make a profit by producing something of benefit to customers. Investors receive their share of these profits in the form of dividends or increases in the value of the stock. Further, when the stock becomes sold, both buyer and seller agree on the price. There is no wager–no prior agreement to risk loss at another's expense. If either thinks the price is unfair, they refuse to deal. (It may be possible to gamble or sin in the stock market, but buying stock does not inherently make up gambling.)

Buying insurance. Some think insurance is gambling. But again, there is no wager and there is compensation. No one agrees to gain at the expense of someone else's loss. On the contrary, the whole purpose of insurance is to compensate the insured if he does have a loss (such as death, or car wreck). If no such loss occurs, the customer has bought peace of mind knowing he would have become rewarded if he had experienced a loss. Regardless of whether this is a wise investment, the point here is that it is not gambling. *The gambler always wants financial loss to occur, because he hopes to profit from those losses.*

ACTIVITIES THAT ARE GAMBLING

In the following examples, all the appearances of gambling are present.

• Casino gambling: slot machines, roulette wheels, dice and card games, and number games played for stakes.

• Racetrack betting on horses, dogs.

• Lotteries.

• Charity and church-sponsored bingo, and raffles. If someone says, "It's for a good cause," then just present a gift and skip the gambling!

• Bazaar and fair booths where you pay to spin a wheel and try to win a prize.

• Amateur gambling including poker games for money, office pools, and matching quarters for cokes or coffee, playing marbles for keeps.

• Gambling operator–"the lottery thrives on the fact that a "sucker" is born every minute."

• Even if small amounts of money are involved, such behavior still violates Bible principles. Further, they set a precedent that makes it impossible for one time and again to object to other people's gambling. Where do you draw the line and say, "This much money risked is all right, but any more is immoral?"

The Bible sanctions only three legitimate ways for money or possessions to pass from one owner to another. Gambling fits none of them.

1. The law of labor ("the work ethic")

One paid as compensation for work done to produce goods or services that benefit other people.

Scripture strongly teaches this "work ethic." The laborer is worthy of his wages (1 Tim. 5:18; Luke 10:7). Do not steal but labor at good (useful) work (Eph.4: 28). To meet our needs, we should do our own business and work for an income (not take what other people earned) (1 Thess. 4:11-12; Matt. 20:1-15; James 5:4). Like Paul, people should work so they can eat their own bread (not other people's bread) (2 Thess. 3:10-12). If they will not work, they should not eat. We must not try to live off the labors of others. We can expect goods or services from others only as compensation for work we do that produces something of benefit (that which is good–Eph. 4:28). Gambling undermines the Biblical work ethic because, instead of doing productive labor that benefits others, the gambler seeks to get something for nothing by taking what other people have earned.

2. The law of exchange

A person may simply agree to exchange possessions (goods or money) with someone else. Each party paid or compensated when receiving possessions of fair value in return for what he gives up. Bible examples are: Abraham bought a field and a cave for money (Gen. 23:1-18). A merchant sold possessions to buy a pearl (Matt. 13:45-46). The disciples of Jesus traveled to the city to buy food (John 4:8). Note that, in a fair transaction, both parties receive what they view as fair value compared to what they give up. Neither party should try to take other people's property without giving fair value in exchange. But again gambling does not fit here, because the winner has no design to compensate the loser. In fact, each gambler hopes other people will lose so he can take their property, while he hopes no one will take his property. This violates the law of exchange (Gen. 33:19; Prov. 31:16; Acts 4:34,37).

3. The law of giving

A person may knowingly choose, of his own free will, unconditionally giving something away as an expression of good will or kindness, with no duty for the receiver to offer any compensation in return. Bible examples are: Ephesians 4:28–One who has earned goods by his own labor, may choose to give to others in need (2 Cor. 9:6-7). We should give willingly and cheerfully, not grudgingly. Note: If gambling fits this, then we should all gamble bountifully! Acts 20:35–It is more blessed to give than to receive. Do gamblers consider giving to be more blessed than receiving? Giving must come by love, compassion, and need to help others (1 John 3:17-18; 1 Cor. 13:3). Is this what motivates gamblers? No, they agree to give (if they lose) only because they want to win what others have! Again, gambling does not fit this category because gamblers do not give willingly, freely, as an act of love or compassion.

Serving as minister in the Lord's church for three decades has bought the previous addictions to my attention with personal stories from church members. Time and again hearing Christians enter my office stating, "I cannot stop using this drug, this gambling .

habit, alcohol, and the unlawful relationship that is tearing my family apart. Obsessive and addictive behavior is a cancer on society, our community, the church, and our souls (Rom. 6:23).

CONCLUSION

Addictive behavior has caused untold damage, not only financially and temporally, but also spiritually. Christians must obey the civil law (Rom. 13:1-7; 1 Peter 2:13-15). Choices will come to bear when faced with these serious matters: We are either the slave or the master when it comes to addictive behavior. How will friends and Christians reply to this serious problem? We must mirror the example of Jesus and walk in his steps accordingly (1 Pet. 2:21-22; Matt. 10:24-25; 1 Cor. 11:1). Can you honestly imagine Jesus playing a slot machine, indulging in the use of alcohol, illegal drugs and so forth? Honestly now, does this harmonize with the example of Jesus and the teaching of His word?

TOPICS FOR DISCUSSION

1. The 'addictions' that many face is caused by a lack of temperance. Why is being temperate so important in view of the addictions that people face?

2. What causes one to become an addict? What flags should we look for to identify addictive behavior?

3. What two outlets promotes sexual behavior? Sexual addictions is caused by many things, name one.

4. Name the number one drug problem today. Why should social drinking be opposed?

5. Define gambling. Name some common activities that do not fit the definition of gambling. What are some specific things done that fits the mold of gambling?

Chapter Thirteen

Testing Our Faith

13

eeting the challenges of life is a difficult proposition to all and depends on faith and resilience as we face the crisis that lies ahead. The loss of a job, home, or even the failure to preserve one's marriage, and keeping the family together can become a difficult mountain to climb. Misfortunes and difficulties that we face in life will try our souls, but remembering that God is in control is satisfying to know. Paul says God comforts us in all our distress. The apostle faced stoning, stripes, prison, shipwreck, robbers, perils, and death (2 Cor. 11:22-23). The apostle admitted God calling him on to his side, which is the literal meaning of comfort (2 Cor. 1:3-7). The word comfort combines the thoughts of encouragement with alleviation of grief.

Paul said his fear pushed him to the edge of endurance. The apostle reached a vulnerable state at Corinth leaving himself bare without any one on which to lean, but God. Then, he learned to depend on God and not trust in himself. God delivered him from that circumstance and convinced him He would always deliver him (2 Cor. 1:8-10). Reaching the point of total misery caused Paul to rely on God. He also learned to thank God and others who were praying for him to do the same (2 Cor. 1:11). This writer is deeply humbled to receive the prayers of the righteous, which provide a boost that defies words of explanation (James 5:16).

We have discussed so far troubles and misfortunes that would bring most to the brink of abandoning their faith. Remaining faithful to God and His will is the only sane and sensible approach in overcoming the trials of life. The writer to the Hebrews states: "Without faith it is impossible to please Him..." (Heb. 11:6). Faith is essential in the face of spiritual and physical problems. Time and again we see examples of the faithful managing evil in its various forms. To see those successfully rising from the ashes, while clinging to the anchor of our souls, confirms that faith in God makes all problems possible.

Adversity And Sickness. A test of our faith. Job, the patriarch of the Old Testament, was so desperate for comfort that he regretted his birth and wanted to die. Still, he was faithful and eventually appeared victorious. One has suggested the jeweler, who works on jewelry or precious stones, may test the genuineness of a stone by applying fire to the gem. Only in this way can the impurities become detected and expel the inferior from the genuine. Jewelers who take their craft seriously will not pass off an imitation for the real and genuine; neither will the Christian presume to be something he is not. The apostle Paul said, "Every man's work shall be made manifest... because it shall be revealed by fire and the fire shall try every man's work of what sort it is" (1 Cor. 3:13). The burning fires of that day, Paul says, shall reveal the character of everyone, as fire sheds light revealing the impurities before hidden, but now reveals the integrity of the real. God even tested the genuineness of Job by his trials before putting him away safely in His care.

Job did not understand why he suffered (Job 42:1-6). There are times when we need reminding that we do not know the mind of God. His lofty ways are far beyond our understanding (Rom. 11:33-36). When Job's suffering ended God gave him twice as much as he had before. Seven more sons and three more daughters blessed this home while his wealth increased dramatically (Job 42:10-17). This faithful patriarch was blessed by God and was easily described as, "Joy comes in the morning" (Psm. 30:5).

Sorrow And Bereavement. A test of faith. There is no greater test, to which we may subject ourselves than facithe loss of a friend or family member. This author with scores of others reading these lines, has experienced great loss and bereavement at some point during life. Such emptiness describes all of us with a hollow feeling that defies human speech. The apostle Paul depicts the body as a tabernacle (tent), which was a temporary house place (2 Cor. 5:1). The child of God has his citizenship in Heaven, and longs for the permanent home he will have there (Phil. 3:20). We must have a panoramic view of life, knowing that we long for an everlasting body. "For in this we groan, earnestly desiring to be clothed upon with our house which is from Heaven: If so being clothed we shall not be found naked" (2 Cor. 5:2-3). Christians do not look forward to death, but conversely long for that immortal life beyond death (2 Cor. 5:4). Remember, Christ promised to go and prepare a place for His disciples. He also promised to come again to take them to that prepared place (John 14:1-6).

True believers know that death is not the end, but a transition to our real home. Peter writes: "Dearly beloved, I beg you as strangers and pilgrims, to abstain from fleshly lusts, which war against the soul" (1 Peter 2:11). The word, "pilgrims" from the Greek word "parepideemous" suggests "one who travels a distance from his own country to visit a holy place; a traveler or wanderer." The meaning is that Christians have no permanent home on this earth. Their citizenship is not here, but are mere sojourners passing through to that heavenly home. Since this land is not our home we must not form any attachments that would take our eye off that blissful place which God has created. The child of God knows the dead will change in a moment and in a twinkling of an eye. The trump of God will ring out causing our bodily tabernacle to give way to an immortal body prepared for eternity (1 Cor. 15:54-57).

Clarence McCartney once quoted Francis Bacon: "Men fear death as children fear to go in the dark."

Then he added: "My own experience at many deathbeds has been death is its own sedative and removes fear in the mind of dying. But because so many dread that last experience in life, it will always be true the fearful will die many times. The Christian facing death should be the last one to fall victim of fear. David said: "Yea, though I walk through the valley of the shadow of death, I will fear no evil: for thou art with me; thy rod and thy staff they comfort me" (Psm. 23:4)

Discouragement–A test of faith. There was once a soldier that became subject to a court-martial, not for treason or consorting with the enemy, but for demoralizing the troops. This soldier, mingling with the troops, was constantly undermining those fighting for a just cause. The attitude of this single soldier was able to discourage this company of men and eventually caused fear and panic, which made them ill-prepared for waging war. A court-martial became necessary to remove such a source of discouragement before battle took place. We face our own individual wars. However one person can bring discouragement and fear that will bring paralysis to us when engaged with battles of our own.

As a child, a booster shot often became necessary as a follow-up to vaccinations originally given, which gave us a better opportunity to withstand childhood diseases. It is equally true that Christians need to have a booster shot when facing problems that would threaten their faith. Those who are in danger of fainting or need spiritual strengthening must give attention to our spiritual medical book, the Bible. The Hebrew writer cautioned his readers that they were weak and needed to grow stronger. "Ye have need that one teach you again, which be the first principles of the oracles of God and have need of milk and not of (meat) solid food" (Heb. 5:12). The inspired writer continues "For everyone that useth milk is unskillful in the word of righteousness: for he is a babe. But strong meat (food) belongeth to them that are of full age" (Heb. 5:13-14). Discouragement is a spiritual problem resolved only through a dose of God's word. An individual once said, "Encouragement is like premium gasoline: it helps to take the knocks out of living." A failure to provide support and encouragement for those in need will cause a chance of driving him from the right road because of a lack of encouragement. It will also deprive us of a rare privilege to help a weak brother (Gal. 6:1).

Doubt And Indecision. A test of faith. Webster defines doubt as "uncertain, fear, lack of confidence, or faith." Doubt and indecision have caused many, not the least of which, Christians to fail in life's challenges. Jesus taught his disciples to fear not or they would succumb to their doubt. To the dithering Peter, Jesus said: "O thou of little faith, wherefore didst thou doubt?" (Matt. 14:31). Peter was rash, impulsive, and hasty in his behavior, but easily daunted and prone to fall. He was afraid and overwhelmed by the sea; he cried for help. Jesus thus reached out and saved the emotional disciple from drowning. So often people lose their balance and fail to make the right choices .

which will change their lives and their soul will weigh in the balance.

The stirring gospel hymn tells us, "Faith is the victory that overcometh the world." The Hebrew writer states: "Without faith it is impossible to be well pleasing to him" (Heb. 11:6). However, faith is much more than a mere step in God's plan of salvation. Faith is the substance, that under girding power that motivates the Christian's entire being. This indispensable virtue comes through the word of God (Rom. 10:17). Bear in mind that our faith grows in part to our zeal, enthusiasm, and the spiritual enlightenment. This growing period comes through the qualities that we often call the Christian graces (2 Peter 1:5-10). The faith is the formula that overcomes doubt and confusion. The lack of faith causes many negative reactions. For example:

• There are more than 600,000 Americans in mental hospitals across our nation.

• In Texas nearly $100,000 of taxpayers money goes for the mentally ill.

• Americans spend 40 to 50 million dollars yearly for tranquilizers to overcome anxiety.

The doubt and indecision that permeates the lives of Christians contributes to the spiritual depression that exists today. Taking tranquilizers and barbiturates just compounds the problem as the drug scourge continues to deepen in our society. Fear is nothing new to our nation. President Franklin D. Roosevelt, in 1932, made a striking statement in a joint session of Congress, "The greatest thing we have to fear is fear itself." Those words are true within the political or spiritual framework. Paul declares: "For God hath not given us the spirit of fear; but of power, and of love, and of a sound mind" (2 Tim. 1:7). If God did not produce fear in our hearts, it seems obvious that Satan did. Faith is the cure that overcomes our doubts and indecision. The single way to defeat the enemy of our soul is to "Put on the shield of faith" (Eph. 6:16).

CONCLUSION

There are times when our faith is weak, and that weakness leads us to question God's concern in our lives. If we would come to a fuller knowledge of God's will and a deeper understanding, it will enable us to have fewer doubts. Let us remember, "God is our refuge and strength, a very present help in trouble"(Psm. 46:11). David cried out, "Trust in him at all times; ye people, pour out your heart before him: God is a refuge for us" (Psm. 62:8).

TOPICS FOR DISCUSSION

1. Why does the jeweler apply heat to precious stones? Similarly does God use the same method to decide genuineness of His people? Why does it work?

2. What is the meaning of the word "pilgrims" and why is it important in the trials we face on earth?

3. In what way is 'discouragement' a hindrance to the Christian? What is the cure of such a condition?

4. How does doubt reveal itself in our society? What is the resolution to this problem?

Chapter Fourteen

Suicide:
A Christian Viewpoint

14

Have you ever considered taking your own life? If not, you are in the minority. This thought has crossed the minds of 90% of Americans according to studies taken. **Newsweek**, a national publication, reported a few years ago that a book on the market, "**A Guide to Self—Deliverance**" depicted the details on how to commit suicide, an alternative for the terminally ill. The calamity of our culture has taken another leap in their contempt for human life. Suffering from a devastating disease, multiple sclerosis has caused me to evaluate how precious life is. Taking my life has never been a consideration on my worst day. Almost two years ago a Christian whom I have known said, "Bob, have you ever thought about suicide?" Replying to this Christian without showing my anger, I said, "There has never been one day when such a thought ever crossed my mind." Speaking to this person gently without provoking her, it became obvious that she needed further teaching on the subject. Information came to us later that this weak person had entertained the idea. How sad to think our problems can only be solved by the senseless act of suicide.

Traditionally, Judaism, Roman Catholic and Protestant theologians have agreed that God condemns the act of suicide. Augustine and Thomas Aquinas stated that murder or taking your own life was in violation of the sixth commandment (Exod. 20:13). Joseph Fletcher, a social ethicist and author of **Situation Ethics, Morals and Medicine and the Ethics of Genetic Control,** contributed enormously to removing moral absolutes and made a defense of euthanasia (mercy killing) in his writings. This produced an atheistic tendency in our nation producing unbelief. Lacking belief in God creates an atmosphere that produces relativism making suicide and other acts acceptable. This attitude permeates every part of life making it essential to follow the fundamental truths embedded in Holy Scripture. Consideration of suicide will not happen with a strong foundation of God's Word in our hearts.

Biblical Foundation Against the Crime of Suicide – stating it expressly, there is no specific law against the crime of suicide. However, taking one's life goes against the whole prohibition against destroying that which God created. Contrary to the practice and the philosophy of paganism, the act became a deep abhorrence by the Hebrews because of the high value placed on human life (Matt. 10:28). How inexcusable .

for any but the most deluded and misguided soul to do harm to their own bodies. Only the shameful and those blinded by sorrow could drive one to commit such an act, as King Saul (1 Sam. 31:4) and Judas (Matt. 27:5) (**International Standard Bible Encyclopedia**).

1 Samuel 31:4 – Saul called on his armor bearer to help him by running him through with a sword, but the servant would not, "for he was sore afraid. Therefore Saul took a sword, and fell upon it."

Matthew 27:4-5 – Judas casting the thirty pieces of silver to the chief priests and elders, saying, "I have sinned against innocent blood. And he cast down the pieces of silver in the temple, and departed, and went and hung himself."

The well-known characters above are documented and recognized as those guilty of committing the grievous sin of suicide. Ending one's life regardless of the merit gives no one the right in taking away the gift that God has celebrated as vital.

Strong Statements from Holy Scriptures Banning Suicide:

Romans 14:7-8 "For none of us liveth to himself and no man dieth to himself. For whether we live, we live unto the Lord; and whether we die, we die unto the Lord: whether we live therefore, or die, we are the Lord's."

1 Corinthians 6:19 "What? know ye not that your body is the temple of the Holy Ghost which is in you, which ye have of God, and ye are not your own?"

Ephesians 5:29 "For no man ever yet hated his own flesh; but nourisheth and cherisheth it, even as the Lord the church."

Exodus 20:13 "Thou shalt not kill."

DOCTOR DEATH GIVING RISE TO ASSISTED SUICIDE

The morality of suicide has brought all of us to face the right or wrong of this difficult issue. Dr. Jack Kevorkian, well-known suicide proponent, stated in a speech, "The medical, religious, journalistic and legal communities will not stop me." The self-professed doctor of assisted suicide victims said, "Pass any law you want, I don't care." Dr. "Death" has helped 33 people die since 1990, and also claims that the last patient he aided wasn't sick. How does one determine whether suicide, personally implemented — or otherwise assisted, is a moral act or not? Simply, if human life is merely a freak of nature — a mere accident — then man may dispose of it freely at will. If we are but a conglomeration of living cells, in the same way a roach is, then human life occupies no unique place in the vicinity of earth. In such a case, who has the right to say when it will or will not continue? You and I have not the right to make such a decision.

Those absorbed by such an anti-God philosophy will travel the winding road of life without a moral compass to make decisions as we face the absolutes established by God's Word (Psm. 119:89; Matt. 24:35). The philosophical and humanistic person will have little tolerance for those of us adhering to the strict position of God as the source of life. The only logical conclusion is this: Some superior intellect, outside the earth's environment comes into view as the origin of life, or we have evolved over billions of years. My friends, life did not just happen - it came into existence by the design of a Creator (Heb. 3:4; 11:3; Rom. 1:20).

This is the very affirmation of the Holy Scriptures. The origin of life comes from the "living God," our Creator. In the speech to the Athenian philosophers Paul declared: "[God] himself gives to all life, and breath, and all things." Again, "In him we live, and move, and have our being..." (Acts 17:25, 28; cf. 1 Tim. 6:13). The birth of Christ became undeniably prophesied centuries earlier (Gen. 3:15, 49:10; Isa. 7:14). Moses wrote: the "Lord God formed man of the dust of the ground and breathed in his nostrils the breath of life; and man became a living soul" (Gen. 2:7). Inasmuch as man is not the author of life, he is not autonomous over the soul, and does not have the right to determine when life should become terminated.

The Bible does not sanction the notion of human "autonomy." The word "autonomy" means "self-governing, or independent." Man does not possess self-rule in moral ethics. He is not the source of moral law. Rather, he is subject to the law of God Almighty.

Consider the following facts:

1. God is the Creator of humankind (Gen. 1:26-27). The Psalmist declared that it was the Lord who made us; not we ourselves (Psm. 100:3). Accordingly, we do not own ourselves.

2. As our Maker, God has a right over His creation. Paul asked the question: "Does not a potter have a right over the clay?" (Rom. 9:21). The Creator has the right to instruct us regarding the value of human life.

3. When one presumes to take another's life, without authority from God to so do, he usurps the role of deity; he thus functions as a rebel.

Tragically, our culture is slipping away from the moral precepts of the Scriptures. "Life" has become an expendable concept. More than 1.5 million unborn babies are slaughtered each year in this country. The approximate number of suicides per year is 35,000 men, women, and teens that have determined life is no longer worth living. Either exterminating a million and a half innocent babies per year, or taking one's life by way of suicide robs the Creator of life. We must not cast aside human life as though it belongs to a garbage heap. The soul of America has reached the chasm of eradicating life as we know it, or preserving life as God expects us to do. Every person who reveres God must speak out for the sacredness of human life.

PROMINENT SUICIDES

Suicide of Jews at Masada. According to Josephus, the first-century Jewish historian writes of the account of Masada. The Roman Governor Silva led his 15,000 soldiers at the base of the rock of Masada and began a siege of the fort. The troops erected a siege tower and ramps leading to the fortress wall. Using a fiery battering ram, the Romans attacked the fortress walls. The Jews occupying Masada under the leadership of Eleazar ben Yair became aware of their certain defeat. Confronted by the prospect of surrendering to a hated enemy and becoming their slaves, the Jews decided to die and remain free. 960 men, women, and children committed suicide rather than become the physical and moral slaves of the Romans. Their statement was inescapable, leaving no room to doubt because of their death. The Romans found the Jews and their possessions destroyed, but their food supplies still intact.

Jonestown mass suicide. November 18, 1978, Jim Jones destroyed the People's Temple as he defined it, as this mesmerizing cult leader persuaded his flock to commit the final act of loyalty. Rev. Jones (so-called) considered himself a reincarnation of both Jesus and Lenin, and had visions of impending nuclear holocaust. In 1977, he led his followers to Guyana, in South America, and created his dream community, named Jonestown, in the jungle. Two years later his utopia allegedly worsened into a nightmare when he ordered 638 adults and 276 children to drink juice laced with cyanide poison. Those who resisted or tried to escape from this religious sect suffered death, and Jones himself died of a bullet wound to the head. Jim

Jones, the cult leader, programmed his followers with repeated mock sessions preparing them for the day when the event would take place. How tragic that almost 1,000 men, women, and children blindly followed a blind guide to commit the final act of suicide. Allowing a charismatic person or any one to have such a hold over us will spell sadness and devastation most every time. This act of suicide is a heartbreaking sin not only to the offender but those closest to them. Paul wrote, "For we must all appear before the judgment seat of Christ; that every one may receive the things done in his body, according to that he hath done, whether it be good or bad (2 Cor. 5:10).

Mass suicide near San Diego. The bodies of 39 young men who became part of a religious group died on March 27, 1997. Authorities discovered the bodies in a $1.6 million dollar estate in Rancho Santa Fe, an exclusive community about 20 miles north of San Diego. The victims were all reported to be between 18 and 24 years old and found in various rooms of the mansion. The bodies were in a repose position dressed in white robes, hands at their side, and part of the Heaven's Gate religious cult. The Coroner's office noted that many bodies after examination had become castrated, which has become routine in cases of the occult. Apart from wearing uniform robes, purple shrouds covered the victims. Heaven's Gate leader Applewhite insisted that all members pay for their obedience by divesting themselves of all financial assets. The cult leader had a hypnotic-like hex on the followers that were vulnerable and needy.

Applewhite himself compared their obedience of a "good" religious disciple to that of a "good" dog. This cult leader, master of psychology and mind control, told his followers that he would soon die of cancer (according to the coroner's postmortem, he did not have cancer at all). If his supporters would follow him in death, a <u>UFO</u>, supposed to escort the Hale-Bopp comet, would come and take them away.

NOTE: When we give-up our free will and decision making to others without a serious investigation of the basics of such belief we become easy prey to those willing and able to take advantage. Thirty-nine victims willingly surrendered to an unscrupulous leader becoming victims of their own need. Anyone looking for a utopia or magic potion will most often travel a path leading to heartache and destruction. Freedom of choice comes to us from God and never should we abandon such a gift. Our souls will easily become duped and deluded when we allow one to deceive us from obedience to God (2 Thess. 2:10-12).

SUICIDES OF THE RICH AND FAMOUS

Some of the most recognized names and family members in television, movies, authors and philosophers have decided life was not worth living. Take note of the following: Marilyn Monroe, Brian Keith, Freddie Prinze, John Belushi, Chris Farley, Judy Garland, and River Phoenix are movie stars taking their lives.

Ernest Hemingway, Socrates, Vincent van Gogh, and Judas Iscariot surrendered their lives. The sons and daughters of the following stars gave-up on life: Art Linkletter, Mary Tyler Moore, James Arness, Paul Newman, and Gregory Peck. The pressure and stress that many feel cause them to look in all the wrong places for the answer to life's problems. Jesus underscores life's importance, "For what is a man profited, if he shall gain the whole world, and lose his own soul? Or what shall a man give in exchange for his soul?" (Matt. 16:26).

The Savior of the world lays down the simplicity of salvation. Jesus said, "I am the way, the truth, and the life: no man cometh to the Father, but by me" (John 14:6; Acts 4:12). Coming to accept this fundamental truth will bring happiness that cannot come from worldly enticements (1 Peter 2:11).

FACTS ABOUT SUICIDE

During the last four decades on average 35,000 Americans commit suicide yearly. Sadly, 500,000 people try this deadly act every year. 50,000 young people make a serious effort to commit suicide yearly.

Groups with the highest risks: alcoholics, drug addicts, homosexuals, mental illness, and those with impulsive natures. Individuals become high percentage victims who have these personality traits.

Studies have shown that once every minute a person in the U.S. tries to kill himself with a conscious intent. The **New York Times** reported that 30 million people get professional help for mental problems costing 13 billion dollars. **Note**: the first suicide prevention center was founded in 1958 at Los Angeles, California.

• Most popular press articles suggest a link between the winter holidays and suicides (Annenberg Public Policy Center of the University of Pennsylvania 2003). However, this claim is just a myth. In fact, suicide rates in the United States are lowest in the winter and highest in the spring (CDC 1985, McCleary and others. 1991, Warren, etc. 1983).

• Suicide took the lives of 30,622 people in 2001 (CDC 2004).

• Suicide rates are broadly higher than the national average in the western states and lower in the eastern and midwestern states (CDC 1997).

• In 2002, 132,353 individuals entered emergency rooms and hospitals following suicide efforts; 116,639 survived treatment in emergency departments and released (CDC 2004).

• In 2001, 55% of suicides came by firearm (Anderson and Smith 2003).

GROUPS AT RISK

Males

• Suicide is the eighth leading cause of death for all U.S. men (Anderson and Smith 2003).

• Males are four times more likely to die of suicide than females (CDC 2004).

• Suicide rates are highest among Whites and second highest among American Indian and Native Alaskan men (CDC 2004).

• Of the 24,672 suicide deaths reported among men in 2001, 60% involved the use of a firearm (Anderson and Smith 2003).

Females

• Women report trying suicide during their life-time about three times as often as men (Krug et al. 2002).

Youth

The rate of youth suicides has tripled since the 1950s, and today. Suicide is the third leading cause of death for 15 to 24 year-olds. In 1998, more teenagers and young adults died of suicide than from cancer, heart disease, AIDS, birth defects, stroke, pneumonia, influenza, and severe lung disease combined.

The overall rate of suicide among youth has declined slowly since 1992 (Lubell, Swahn, Crosby, and Kegler 2004). However, rates remain unacceptably high. Adolescents and young adults often experience stress, confusion, and depression from conditions occurring in their families, schools, and communities. Such feelings can overwhelm young people and lead them to consider suicide as a "solution." Few schools and communities have suicide prevention plans to address this relentless problem.

• Suicide is the third leading cause of death among young people ages 15 to 24. In 2001, 3,971 suicides numbered in this group (Anderson and Smith 2003).

• Of the total number of suicides among ages 15 to 24 in 2001, 86% (3,409) were male and 14% (562) were female (Anderson and Smith 2003).

• American Indian and Alaskan Natives have the highest rate of suicide in the 15 to 24 age group (CDC 2004).

• In 2001, firearms became the means used in 54% of youth suicides (Anderson and Smith 2003).

RISK CAUSES RECOGNIZING THE SUICIDAL

The first step in preventing suicide is to identify and understand the risk causes. A specific act that contributes harm to an individual is a risk that we should avoid. However, risk causes alone will not remove this serious and many times deadly act. Research has identified the following risk causes for suicide (DHHS 1999):

• History of mental disorders, principally depression.
• History of alcohol and substance abuse.
• Family history of suicide.
• Family history of child maltreatment.
• Feelings of hopelessness.
• Impulsive or aggressive tendencies.
• Barriers to accessing mental health treatment.
• Loss (relational, social, work, or financial).
• Physical illness.
• Easy access to lethal methods.
• Unwillingness to seek help because of the stigma attached to mental health and substance abuse disorders or suicidal thoughts.
• Cultural and religious beliefs—for instance, the belief that suicide is a noble resolution of a private difficulty.
• Local outbreak of suicide.
• Isolation, a feeling of separation from other people.

MYTHS ABOUT SUICIDE

We have all heard about myths because of the terrible problem of suicide. Let us separate myth and fiction from fact. Coming to grips with the cold, hard facts while grasping the underlying truths in Holy Scripture. Examine the following six myths and the facts about them:

A. MYTH - "people talk about killing themselves, but never do it." Most of us have heard of those making such a statement and some never complete such a terrible deed.

FACT – many people and Christians included, have heard those make either vocally, or by writing a brief avowal their plan to do away with themselves. If they do not follow through with their objective it should serve as a red flag that such a person is crying for help. It may surprise you that 80% of all completed suicides do speak of their plans before. Remember, we are not psychics and do not have a crystal ball. Anyone that would make such a serious statement deserves our attention and concern. Suicide "hot lines" across the nation report thousands "crying for help." These facts alone should highlight the myth and facts about this serious issue.

B. MYTH – "all people who make the effort to commit suicide are fully intent on dying." This myth would seem a predetermined act by the person going to such measures carrying out this deed. Those individuals going to all the trouble in planning such a calculated act appears firm in their decision. However, such may not be accurate when we look beneath the surface and see what troubles live in this disturbed heart.

FACT – we should take note that suicide endeavors surpass completed suicides 10 to 1. This would signal mixed emotions in the inner psyche of those considering such an act. The sobering statistics would point out the person has mixed motives showing the individual has questions and doubt about the rash judgment made. In whatever way you phrase it, this poor victim is crying for help, hoping someone will hear and come to their rescue.

C. MYTH – "only a psychotic or crazy person can in fact go through with suicide." Countless suicide victims go to extreme lengths and well-thought-out strategies to carry out such a deed. Let us not think for one moment that a "crazy person" is the only one qualified to achieve the final act.

FACT – the leading experts are fierce in their denial of the statement. Many suicides come to conclusion by those whose minds have reached the height of their mental powers. We do not wish to offer the names of those committing suicide. However, the following categories would show the high degree of intelligence, such as: Christian professors, elders and preachers in the church, philosophers, and CEO's of huge businesses have ended their lives for reasons that defy understanding.

D. MYTH – "suicide, an inherited disease runs in certain families." This myth has no basis in fact. Those that promote this myth come from folklore without data or proof.

FACT – we should remember that suicide occurs on all levels of society; this shocking act takes place in the slums of Watts or Harlem and conversely in the city of angels (Hollywood) or Wall Street. It can happen to anyone, anywhere regardless of social standing, prestige, or financial skill. None are immune to this devastating act with all races, religions, and sexual gender becoming the target of Satan's trickery. Reminder, the highest total of suicides taking place in the U.S. falls in the 20-24 age group.

E. MYTH – "every victim committing suicide will always leave a note."

FACT – studies have shown that only 15% of completed suicides leave notes; this is in contrast to the stereotypical suicides of television and the movies. Investigations of alleged suicide scenes seldom come to resolution because of the absence of a "so-called" suicide note. Since a note rarely appears confirming death by the hands of the victim; authorities hesitate to reveal the cause as nothing more than an accident by misadventure. Suicide is commonly a spontaneous and irrational act as the person will not always logically think this matter through by crafting a note before taking his life.

BIBLICAL SUICIDES AND DEPRESSION THINKING:

ACTS OF SUICIDE –

Ahithophel, the counselor of King David becomes close to the king with his name appearing 17 times (1 Chron. 27:33). The name "Ahithophel" originates from the Hebrew word meaning, "brother of foolishness."

Ahithophel had a reputation of shrewdness and wisdom; however, he did not show this by joining Absalom's conspiracy to overthrow David and his kingdom. This scheme did not materialize and seeing the plan fall apart Ahithophel avoided certain execution and committed suicide (2 Sam. 17:23).

Zimri – the origin of his name meant, "Wild sheep," or "wild goat," and served as the 5th king of Israel for 7 days (1 Kings 16:15).

Elah, son of Baasha, the 4th king of Israel ruled for two years and became known for his corruption and drunkenness. Elah drinking himself to a drunken state of unconsciousness became vulnerable to Zimri. Zimri, a military strong man, conspired and murdered Elah. Removing King Baasha and the royal family left the dynasty and government with no stability making it easy for *Zimri* to rule the kingdom. These acts of insurgency show the truth that "they who take the sword shall perish with the sword." The conspiracy of *Zimri* lacked the support of the people and his short reign as a king of Israel came to a swift end. The wicked king set fire to the palace with his own hands, and perished in the flames (I Kings 16:18). The short reign of *Zimri* became a blot on the record of these evil men. Becoming destroyed by the deeds of violence eventually drove him to become just as wicked by committing suicide (**ISBE**).

King Saul – Saul's rejection by God traces back to the king's failure to comply in obedience (1 Sam. 15:3). Failing to give full obedience brought down Saul as king (1 Sam. 15:26). Samuel, by God's command, secretly anointed David and consequently the spirit of the Lord left Saul (1 Sam. 16). An evil spirit came on him bringing about madness. Enraged by jealousy the king became obsessed with killing David. The preoccupation with killing David left the kingdom in jeopardy. An army of the Philistines swarmed Saul and his vulnerable nation. Saul's army was crushed, and three of his sons, including Jonathan, were killed. Wounded in the battle, Saul committed suicide by falling on his own sword (1 Sam. 31:4). (**Nelson's Illustrated Bible Dictionary**).

Saul's life is a vivid picture of decline and deterioration until suicide draws a dark curtain over the scene. Rebellion highlights the king's failure to give full obedience to God (1 Sam. 15). Substituting obedience with disobedience will drive one to make wrong decisions. Saul began with humility and a wholehearted desire to serve when suddenly his good heart made a transition to selfishness and a clear abandoning of his duty to serve God.

Abimelech – after Gideon's death the Israelites fell once more into the Baal-worship which Gideon had rooted out from his father's city (Judg. 6:25ff). Israel now in full apostasy worships Baal-berith as their God (Judg. 9:46). Abimelech, son of Gideon (Judg. 9:1), sought the throne of king after the death of his father. Abimelech's taste for power led him to unscrupulous acts and ruled Israel for three short years (verse 22). He won the support of his mother's family and received their recommendation and that of all Israel (vs. 3-4). He then murdered the sons of his father, seventy in number, at Ophrah, the family home in the tribe of Manasseh (Judg. 9:5-18). However, Jotham the youngest son of Gideon escaped as the remaining sibling (v. 5).

Judges 9:50-54 describes the sad ending of the all too brief reign of this wicked king, Abimelech. This evil man went from Shechem to the city of Thebez. Abimelech had little trouble overwhelming and taking the city by force. Surrounding the city he discovered a strong tower providing refuge for the men and women shutting themselves in safety. But when Abimelech advanced to the tower and drew near to the door to set it on fire, a woman threw a millstone down upon him from the tower smashing his skull. He called his armor-bearer and said, "Draw thy sword, and slay me, that men say not of me, a woman slew him. And his young man thrust him through, and subsequently died (Judg. 9:54). This act of self-destruction by his attendant underscores the prideful and cowardly man that Abimelech turned out to be. Judges 9:20 sets forth the prediction of Jotham stating the base ingratitude of the people in raising Abimelech up as king, and foretells the retribution which would fall upon both parties.

Judas Iscariot – is the well recognized disciple who betrayed Jesus. Judas was the son of Simon (John 6:71), or of Simon Iscariot (RSV). The term Iscariot, which is used to distinguish Judas from the other disciple named Judas (Luke 6:16; John 14:22; Acts 1:13). Iscariot refers to his hometown of Kerioth, in southern Judah (Josh. 15:25). Thus, Judas was a Judean, the only one of the twelve apostles who was not from Galilee.

The details of Judas' life are sketchy. Because of his betrayal of Jesus, Judas, however, has become more of a mystery. It must be assumed that Jesus saw promise in Judas, or He would not have called him to be a disciple (**Nelson's Illustrated Bible Dictionary**).

Judas became known as the treasurer or he that held the "bag." It became necessary that someone act as a steward of the funds collected, and consequently this duty fell to Judas. The inspired writer sheds light on Judas as "a thief" using it for his own purpose (John 12:4-6; 13:29). The scene at Bethany with Mary anointing Jesus with the priceless ointment shows great sacrifice. However, Judas protested Mary's use of the costly perfume to anoint Jesus (Matt. 26:6-13; Mark 14:3-9). Showing a concern for the poor by selling the alabaster box of ointment only showed his hypocrisy and smallness of spirit that led to the betrayal of Jesus.

Subsequently, Judas met with the chief priests and conspired to betray Jesus for 30 pieces of silver (Matt. 26:14-16). The disciples afterward convened together for the Passover and Jesus knowing that Satan entered Judas' heart said, "One of you shall betray me" (Matt. 26:21). The disciples cried, "Is it I?" (Matt. 26:22, 25). Immediately Judas left the room and met with the high priests and followers to consummate the conspiracy. Judas joined the Jewish leadership with the soldiers and coming upon Jesus in the Garden of Gethsemane said, "Hail, master, and kissed him" (Matt. 26:47-50). Some debate the motivation of Judas for "casting down the pieces of silver in the temple, and went (out) and hanged himself" (Matt. 27:5). Is it due to a contrite heart producing true sorrow for the evil deed done? Paul writes, "For Godly sorrow worketh repentance to salvation," and conversely "worldly sorrow worketh death" (2 Cor. 7:10). It seems the sorrow provoking the outburst from the betrayer stemmed from "worldly sorrow" which "worketh death" (2 Cor. 7:10). This disciple numbered among the twelve walked with Jesus for over three years, yet was morally bankrupt causing him to commit the ultimate act of suicide (Matt. 27:5).

The chief priests took the money cast down by Judas and purchased the potter's field, afterward called "the field of blood." This act fulfilled the prophecy of Zechariah (Zech 11:12-14), which confirmed the writings by Matthew (Matt. 27:3-10). The account given in Acts 1:16-20 is much shorter. It mentions neither Judas' repentance nor the chief priests, but simply states that Judas "obtained a field with the reward of his iniquity; and falling headlong, he burst asunder in the midst, and all his bowels gushed out" (Acts 1:18). What a sad chapter in the life of a disciple that began with such promise. Peter and Judas made serious errors in judgment, and while Peter repented and became the preacher of Pentecost; Judas committed the ultimate act of disgrace. Jesus said concerning Judas, "it had been good for that man if he had not been born" (Matt. 26:24). The crime committed cannot come from any determination of God. It was a violation of all the duties Judas owed God and to the Lord Jesus. This terrible act is summarized by awful ingratitude, detestable covetousness, and a wicked betrayal that defies imagination.

ACTS OF DEPRESSION

Moses – portrayed in the Old Testament as a type of the Prophet raised up "like unto" him (Deut. 18:15, 18). In the New Testament the Prophet "like unto Moses" has come; Christ stands out as the greatest Prophet in all human history. Moses, one of the greatest characters ever depicted in Holy Writ, became exalted as a legendary leader and lawgiver while facing moments of depression.

Background of Numbers 11:4-35 - the people of Israel left Mount Sinai and traveled three days with the Ark of the Covenant leading the procession in a search for a resting place. Moses besieged the Lord God, "Arise, O Lord, and scatter your enemies; let them flee before you" (Num. 10: 35). The people began to complain before the hearing of the Lord and His anger was kindled as fire consumed them in the farthest part of the camp. The complaining about the loss of family members and the displeasure of their food supply reached the ears of Israel's leader. Moses with a heavy heart became overwhelmed with the weeping of the people; the Lord's anger was kindled against the people enormously (Num. 11: 10). Moses manifesting great stress to the Lord, said, "I am not able to bear this people alone; because it is too heavy for me" (Num. 11:14). The overwhelming depression of Moses had reached fervor pitch as he petitioned the Father to kill him. His depression led him to desperate measures and the Lord hearing His servant's cry provided an antidote to his stress. Bringing a formula that will address Moses' anguish came to completion with the selection of "seventy men of the elders of Israel" to help him bear the burden of the people (Num. 11:16-17).

Job - recognized as the faithful patriarch of patience and the epitome of endurance despite the losses he experienced in his life. His physical agony has become well documented, but no one will ever calculate the enormity of pain and humiliation during the test of his faith. Hear Job's cry, "So that my soul chooseth strangling, and death rather than my life. I loathe it; I would not live alway: let me alone; for my days are vanity" (Job 7:15-16). Job, the devoted patriarch, faced stress and depression stemming from the physical agony thrust on him. The stress of Job seems to say that he would prefer even the most violent kind of death to the life that he was then leading (v. 15). Many who face physical illness may become overwhelmed to such an extent they would prefer death over the agony they endure. We all have our weak moments and perhaps this was a momentary lapse in the life of Job. His flesh was wasting away as his body was covered with ulcers and boils.

Job, in his view, thought of himself as a speedily dying man. Perhaps the words of the patriarch had become exaggerated, but in his view death could not come soon enough. Sickness may present itself as a spiritual exercise challenging us to think about death. This reflection during a serious period of sickness will put us in mind of our purpose on this earth. If mindful of resting on the brink of death we may, in faith, come to realize the importance of God, as Job does. Life is short and uncertain while facing the unpredictable prospects of confronting death (James 4:13-14). This faithful man of God confronted the greatest test of his life and feeling he had become a burden to himself preferred death. Job ultimately persevered and became blessed beyond all his dreams. God blessed or rewarded His servant to his former prosperity and doubled in many cases from what he possessed before (Job 42:9-17). We may not always enjoy the blessings of material things, but with confidence will perceive the gifts coming from our Father in heaven. Job never saw the Ten Commandments, the Sermon on the Mount, or hear the sermon on Pentecost, but faithfully followed God. The blessings coming to us as His children will exceed our sincere expectations (Eph. 1:3).

Jonah - cries out, "O Lord, take, I beseech thee, my life from me; for it is better for me to die than to live" (Jonah 4:3). The Lord had previously commissioned Jonah, "Arise, go to Nineveh, that great city, and cry against it; for their wickedness is come up before me" (Jonah 1:2). Nineveh, an Assyrian city of almost 600,000 souls, exhibited great rebellion against God. The message of God's prophet was simple, "Yet forty days, and Nineveh shall be overthrown. So the people of Nineveh believed God, and proclaimed a fast, and put on sackcloth, from the greatest of them even to the least of them" (Jonah 3:4-5). This is the purpose of preaching to produce convictions that bring results. Jonah's concern for the people of Nineveh came to zilch, zero, and desperately wanted the people of Nineveh destroyed. His impatience and disappointment in the city repenting from the highest to the lowest brought Jonah to a state of disillusionment and bitterness.

Jonah, the selected messenger of the Lord was annoyed the city of Nineveh was spared. He prayed that God would take his life from him, as his desire to see Nineveh destroyed did not materialize. Realizing the predicted destruction of Nineveh failed to take place created frustration and rage. This gives us occasion to suspect that Jonah only delivered the message of wrath against the Ninevites, and did not assist or encourage them in their repentance. One might think the prophet of God would use his skill as God's spokesman to kindly persuade his audience to come before God with a contrite heart full of repentance. It seems clear the prophet did not want his audience (Nineveh) to comply with God's message. Conversely, the prophet of the Lord would have taken joy in the total annihilation of Nineveh. Jonah, to my knowledge, was the lone prophet that did not want his audience to give full obedience to the message he preached. What a sad commentary on a prophet or preacher that would derive great satisfaction in seeing his audience reject the divinely appointed message.

The Lord called Jonah's attitude into question, "Then said the Lord, doest thou well to be angry? (Jonah 4:4). In the light of God's concern for man, how could His servant be so ungodly? Jonah's stress and depression coming from such an attitude defies understanding. Placing one's soul in jeopardy by praying to God, "O Lord, take, I beseech thee, my life from me; for it is better for me to die than to live," seems foolish (Jonah 4:3).

Elijah - did not face suicide due to the demands of his work and the testing by God. The heavy demands of his work and the trials of the people caused self-pity and a depressed state. Elijah and his personal character is not affirmed in one concise statement. Conversely, he appears in the biblical account suddenly to the reader while his appearance and disappearance seem just as abrupt. The premise of the Bible is not to give a complete biography of any individual, whether prophet or king, but to display the working of God upon the kingdoms of Israel and Judah through the prophets. Few personal details appear on the pages of the Bible concerning such characters as the prophet Elijah.

Following the events at Mount Carmel with the contest between Elijah and the 450 prophets of Baal; King Ahab informed his wife, Jezebel, that the prophet of God slew the prophets of Baal at the brook of Kishon (I Kings 18:40). Jezebel, the epitome of evil, sent a messenger to Elijah, saying, "So let the gods do to me, and more also, if I make not thy life as the life of one of them by tomorrow about this time" (1 Kings 19:2). Elijah did not have to wait long before the intentions of Queen Jezebel became known. Her design and threat to kill the prophet would come within the space of a day. Elijah traveled about a day and while sitting under a juniper tree, said, "O Lord take away my life; for I am not better than my fathers" (1 Kings 19:4). Jonah like Elijah's depression reached an unprecedented level that caused him to petition the Lord to take his life.

God did not lose sight of His servant, but watched over him, and miraculously ministered to his wants, enabling him to complete his work as the

Lord's prophet. 1 Kings 19:5-8 sets forth the goodness of our Creator by using an angel to feed him in the wilderness. If God had not graciously sustained him, he would have perished. God, all too often, deals with His children better than they deserve! Elijah wanted to die however; God had a mission for the prophet and sent an angel to keep him alive with cakes and water.

SOME CAUSES OF SUICIDE

Dr. Herbert Hendid, "Suicide is a barometer of social tensions."

Encyclopedia Britannica, "Suicide is the companion of a high standard of living, advanced age, and loneliness."

Suicide decreases where a deep religious faith exists and a simple life style.

Studies have shown the breakup of our family structure through the death of a relative or friend often contributes to suicide.

Suicide comes from the loss of a job, income, or business; also the pressure of unbearable anguish, loss of power, or position.

Suicide stems from the loss of one's health, severe pain endured, and either real or imagined malignancy, or the fear of going in sane.

Suicide occurs when relationships crumble between men and women; the breakup of marriage, and friendships.

Suicide is caused by depression when the intensity grows in duration. The third most common health problem in the U.S. is hypertension or anxiety contributing to the widespread problem under consideration.

Suicide often comes from alcohol or drug abuse when withdrawal and other symptoms make it unbearable.

Suicide comes by those practicing martyrdom like terrorists disregarding their own life for a cause.

Suicide is often traced to lives of shame: teenage pregnancy, fraudulent businessman, etc.

CLUES TO IDENTIFY SUICIDE VICTIMS

Most victims are premeditated in this act, rather than done on the impulse.

Three-fourths have seen a doctor within four months of their self-destruction.

Depressed and hopeless are obvious signs: Verbal clues, "My family would be better off," – "This is the last straw."

Victim withdraws from people: reduction in eating habits, and stops talking.

The failure to concentrate and focus on their job and loved ones; unresponsive to family and friends.

Take note of those complaining with aches, pains, and headaches; loss of weight and appetite.

Observe those making out a will, taking out insurance, reviewing finances and giving away special items or possessions.

GIVING COUNSEL TO THOSE ENTERTAINING SUICIDE

Giving assurance to those considering such an act must come to realize their problem can change.

Let us emphasize the individual considering such a crisis may seem permanent, but is only temporary.

Providing encouragement to the subject while persuading them to have a complete medical evaluation would bring some piece of mind. Suicide victims often commit the final act due to health problems. Receiving a full medical examination could remove the cause of such a final act.

The person working with such a desperate soul should offer advise to get help from a professional therapist, physician, preacher, or family member.

Giving the potential suicidal victim encouragement as a friend will help immensely. We cannot underestimate the fundamental act of human kindness and those we genuinely care about.

If possible, arrange for social contact with others which will give interaction to the person considering suicide.

The child of God who wants to live in eternal bliss with all the faithful cannot entertain such a prospect by destroying that which God has given.

Encourage such a person to have fellowship with Christians as most suicidal victims feel lonely and unloved. Galatians 6:2 states "Bear ye one another's burdens and so fulfill the law of Christ."

LESSONS FOR SURVIVING FAMILY

Suicide survivors must learn that a failure to face this unbearable experience may cripple their mental health; consequently it leaves a stigma that will shroud the family life forever. Suicide is a selfish act bringing recriminations to the surviving family lasting for the remainder of their lives. It is a single act never totally forgotten and never totally forgiven.

Suicide is a singular act with a plural effect. Paul provides a divine rule, "God is not mocked: for whatsoever a man soweth, that shall he also reap" (Gal. 6:7). Mocking God will never materialize to our spiritual good. Conversely sowing spiritual things will produce good to our lives, while sowing to the flesh will generate evil things. This is a fundamental truth when one selfishly takes away that which belongs to the Creator and a price is paid. The prophet said, "I will recompense thy ways upon thee, and thine abominations shall be in the midst of thee: and ye shall know that I am the LORD (Ezek. 7:4; Heb. 10:30). Arnold Toynbee, a 19th century historian, states "Deaths sting is two-pronged, and in the allotment of suffering, the survivor takes the brunt."

Communication is the key to surviving together in the aftermath of a suicide.

(1) Verbal communication is the key which involves speaking and listening.

(2) Non-verbal is committed through sight, and touch (Talk about a hug).

(3) Allow God into your situation, He will help you in your weakness through prayer and Bible reading.

(4) Allow the church to care for you – take advantage of worship opportunities

(5) Close the wound in your life, and let it heal over. Remember, a scar will always remain and will become sensitive to the touch (Rom. 15:1). The word "bear" in the larger sense means "feeling indulgent,

or endure patiently."

Depression portrays itself as a consequence for surviving family members.

(1) Normally family members will suffer a depressed state for about 6 months.

Survivors are advised by counselors to avoid isolation and seclusion as a response to an emotional injury. The treatment of grief is best handled while awake and not drugged.

(2) During the depression period often family members will not feel well physically: Nervousness, fatigue, rashes, upset stomach, and distorted vision are symptoms experienced.

Guilt often becomes a normal side-effect to those losing a loved one suddenly.

(1) Who is to blame? Family arguments abound with respect to the blame game. We will never come to a resolution by playing the blame game as it becomes an exercise in futility.

(2) Blaming others: God, parents, employers, doctors, and counselors.

(3) The best therapy for guilt:

    (a) **Confession** – tell the truth about what makes you feel guilty. First of all confess before the God above; confess to family and friends resolving any differences.

    (b) **Forgiveness** – the theme of the Bible is a message of forgiveness. We must all learn this lesson, in particular to forgive ourselves. Surviving family members learning to forgive one another will make a giant step toward reconciliation. Remember the good times and cherish the positive memories you shared.

WHY LIFE SHOULD GO FORWARD

The difficulties of life may seem overwhelming at times when a sudden death or suicide occurs with a special friend or our own family. Regardless of our station in life, rich, poor, young, old, hardships will occur to each of us. Jesus, the great physician knows His patient, man. He is able to provide the perfect prescription, which allows us to cope with the complexities of life. *"Don't Ever Give Up"* is not just a pleasant slogan to the ear, but is the only formula permitting us to meet the hurts and hardships that confront us. The basis or foundation underpinning our lives comes from a belief and practice of the following:

1. Life is a gift from God and highlighting its importance should never be taken for granted. David writes with clarity: "Know ye that the LORD he is God: it is he that hath made us, and not we ourselves; we are his people, and the sheep of his pasture" (Psm. 100:3). Life springs from the everlasting God in heaven and not from the unproved and improvable theory of evolution. Let us remember that God "breathed in his (man) nostrils the breath of life; and man became a living soul" (Gen. 2:7). The crowning achievement of God's handiwork is the creation of man. The Creator had a divine purpose for man and woman to live in happiness and expected obedience in return (Gen. 2:16-17). We must treasure the wonderful gift of life and value each day as though it were our last. James writes, "What is your life? It is as a vapor that appeareth for a little time, and then vanisheth away" (James 4:14). The gift of life is precious and seizing every moment to God's glory should become our sole meaning of life.

2. **We have redemption "in Christ,"** which is the fulfillment of the mystery prearranged in eternity (Eph. 3:3-4, 9). The mystery was hidden or concealed until such time it would come to full view or understanding. Peter gives us a picture of the angels intent on finding out the plan of human redemption, but prevented them from doing so (1 Peter 1:12). Paul writes: "Whereby when you read, you can perceive my understanding in the mystery of Christ" (Eph. 3:4). The sheer reading of the gospel of Christ permits us to have an understanding of the salvation located "in Christ" (Eph. 1:3). In the fullness of time God would reveal His scheme of redemption through Christ (Gal. 4:4).The grand purpose in the creation of the universe stresses the wisdom of God, which might be known in the church (Eph. 3:10-11). God's depth and love for humankind cannot be questioned designing a plan that would bring salvation to the world (Rom. 5:8; Eph. 1:7). John states that Jesus is the "propitiation for our sins: and not for ours only, but also for the sins of the whole world (1 John 2:2). The word "propitiation" may seem like a strange word, but simply means Jesus is the atoning sacrifice for our sins.

Surrendering to God's plan requires full and complete obedience (Matt. 7:21; Heb. 5:8-9). Jesus giving the worldwide commission, said, "Go ye into all the world and preach the gospel to every creature. He that believeth and is baptized shall be saved and he that believeth not shall be damned" (Mark 16:15-16). Paul, the apostle, reiterated the Savior, saying, "For as many of you as were baptized into Christ did put on Christ" (Gal. 3:27). Surviving tragedy of any magnitude will demand we live in accordance to the teachings of Christ.

3. **There is no great tragedy in dying, but the tragedy comes when dying for the wrong reason.** My family and I suffered a great loss when our daughter, Bethany, left our home to buy some stamps at the post office. Sending her on such an errand seems frivolous when looking back, but accidents do occur and her life ended at the tender age of 16. Many of our readers have experienced through family or friends precious loved ones that perish quickly and for no apparent reason. Our daughter on the brink of womanhood had her life cut short, but the knowledge of her life as a Christian give us hope (1 Thess. 4:13-17). We will never erase the hurt of that moment, yet the consolation of her obedience to Christ gives us hope (1 Peter 1:3).

Gospel preachers of my earliest memory eloquently would say, "We are all human beings and after birth we become one day closer to death than the day before." Our stay on this planet is brief and each day lived to the fullest. David of the Old Testament states, "The days of our years are threescore years and ten; and if by reason of strength fourscore years" (Psm. 90:10). Threescore and ten represents 70 . years and perhaps 80 if the Lord wills. If we live 80 to 90 years we would become fortunate, but in the backdrop of eternity it means little. Dying is part of the human dilemma and we cannot escape its painful certainty. The importance of readying ourselves for death is definitive in importance. Note, "And it is appointed unto men once to die, but after this the judgment" (Heb. 9:27). If we will take the time to ponder such biblical characters: Cain, King Saul, Judas, Demas, Agrippa, Ananias and Sapphira and others we will see those dying tragically. The previous persons died without obeying God's precepts, or failing to live according to the commands of the Lord. We would characterize these as dying tragically. Conversely, Abraham, Moses, Peter, Paul, John and others finished their lives in death as faithful servants ready to meet their judge and thrust to that heavenly palace (Rev. 2:10). Life is a gift from God and preparing for death is the most important thing you and I can do as we surge closer to the divine appointment.

4. **For the Christian there is a new way of looking at the world.** Our vision will turn to a clear and insightful approach moving forward with a positive attitude. Life is an exciting adventure when viewed from the Christian perspective. Paul writes to the Corinthians, "Therefore if any man be in Christ, he is a new creature: old things are passed away; behold, all things are become new" (2 Cor. 5:17). This does not mean all our financial obligations will disappear, or personal conflicts with neighbors and friends will fade. Christians will put into practice the basic principles of the New Testament causing the

world to see that we are Christ-like.

Jesus said, "Ye are the light of the world. A city set on a hill cannot be hid," (Matt. 5:14). This basic truth illustrates the example of the Christian in a world permeated with darkness. Christians living in a crooked and perverse world may have a positive impact by lighting up the world in the lives they live (Phil. 2:15). The world offers countless opportunities for Christians making an impact for good. Jesus said, "Love one another as I have loved you; by this shall all men know that ye are my disciples, if ye have love one to another" (John 13:34-35). The world will see that we are His followers by the love we have for fellow Christians. Christianity will have an attractive and appealing feature if we practice the new commandment. Regardless of the circumstances we face, life will go forward as we "press toward the mark for the prize of the high calling of God in Christ Jesus" (Phil. 3:14).

CONCLUSION

Despite the increased standard of living, excellent health care, educational opportunities, suicide continues as a menace to society. We have learned in our study that approximately 35,000 suicides take place yearly in our nation. People look for happiness in all the wrong places and doing so raises questions about the meaning of life. Jesus provides the formula for living life and the remedy for depression goes hand and glove. This brings people to improper conclusions and consequently rash decisions are made. Jesus informs His disciples, "I am come that they may have life, and that they may have it more abundantly" (John 10:10).

Dr. and Mrs. Henry Van Dusen in 1975 committed suicide as both took an overdose of pills. Authorities found a note stating, "Life is no longer worth the struggle, why go on?" This is a tragic commentary about the life of this prominent couple. King David said, "God is our refuge and strength, a very present help in trouble, therefore we will not fear, though the earth be removed, and though the mountains be carried into the city" (Psm. 46:1-2). If faced with life's struggle's we would profit from the penetrating words of David.

When calamity and heartache strikes at our door may we draw strength from our faith in God. When alone and life seems its worst, **"Don't Ever Give Up"** becomes the only sane and sensible approach in confronting the trials of life (James 4:14-17).

THOUGHT QUESTIONS

1. What Scriptures or arguments would you offer to refute those promoting the act of suicide?

2. The mass suicide examples listed have what in common?

3. Name the cited individual cases of suicide and give the strangest.

4. Give the single most important rule for surviving families.

5. What myth about suicide surprised you the most?

Chapter Fifteen

Shocking Events Do Happen

15

The following dates have a special meaning to me and my family: **August 31, 1974,** a senseless murder took the life of my brother producing pain and loss unimaginable. **February 21, 1994,** my saintly mother lost a battle against acute leukemia succumbing to this terrible disease. Her untimely death has left a void among our family. However, her example has inspired us with a legacy of faithfulness that will burn in our hearts forever. **April 21, 1995,** a surgical procedure, spinal fusion, took place on my body and resulted in a failure to walk forcing me to a wheelchair. The sequence of my condition has caused a bedfast state lasting almost ten years to this point. **August 12, 1995,** the Mayo Clinic diagnosed my illness as progressive multiple sclerosis. Four days later, **August 16, 1995,** our daughter, Bethany Ann (16) suffered a terminal automobile accident ending the life of a beautiful Christian girl on the brink of womanhood. Her death challenged us beyond any words eloquently stated. Bethany's infectious laugh and winning smile won the hearts of her family and countless others that knew her. Never will we forget those special memories she left behind and will go with us till we face our divine appointment.

David Johnson, my brother-in-law, died on **August 13, 2002,** from lymphoma in the leukemia stage. David, 60, my sister's deceased husband, left us much too early. He was a wonderful husband, father, and doting grandfather of three girls and a boy. David was never considered an in-law, but simply our brother. The epitome of humility and meekness he served as an elder in two separate congregations. He served as a preacher, Bible school teacher, deacon, and did so faithfully without fanfare or seeking recognition. How desperately we need David's tribe to increase with devotion and commitment to the cause of Christ.

Our family is not the only ones suffering needlessly the loss of family members that has molded and shaped our lives. These events serve as a reminder that such shocking trials do happen. The author of these lines has grappled with agonizing heartbreak, loss, devastation, and having one's health suddenly ripped away. Gospel preachers do not live with their heads in a cloud with the ability to ignore their world crashing around him. Some, if not all, of the anguish expressed above demands enormous strength and stamina to bear. Yet, faith in God with a single-minded loyalty to the Creator and His holy Word compels us to follow His divine compass bringing solace and hope. David pursued by a mad King Saul, said, "God is our refuge and strength, a very present help in trouble. Therefore will not we fear, though the earth be removed, and though the mountains be carried into the midst of the sea" (Psm. 46:1-2). David possessed a wonderful spirit and though faced with an arch enemy discovered the answer lays on the everlasting arm of God (Deut. 33:27).

This compass never fails and will lead us to the ideal place if we faithfully follow the directions. Peter states, "All things that pertain to life and godliness (come) to us through the knowledge of him (God) that called us by his glory and virtue" (2 Peter 1:3).

Reader friend, we have all faced human misfortune and serious problems that cause us to ask, "Why do these shocking events happen?" Predictably we hear the familiar tune, "Why did God do this?" Or, "Why did God let this happen?" These are fitting questions and deserve forthright answers. The Bible, God's Word, is the best possible place to find the answers for life's most perplexing questions.

CAUSES OF EVENTS TRACED TO OUR OWN DOING

All of us have been born in this world screaming and hollering demanding attention and placing the blame of our discomfort on others. One morning following a sermon a Christian man left the assembly outraged. He felt in some way the preacher had become responsible for some of his problems. Later, information surfaced that the brother lost his job as the preacher became an easy target for the man's frustration. Many of our problems and blessings are because of our own actions. A person who eats too much can blame only himself for gaining weight. Developing lung cancer because of heavy cigarette smoking cannot be blamed on anyone else.

The divisive condition between Abraham, Lot, and their respective herdsman produced an impossible environment. Abraham recognized the strife between himself and Lot (Gen. 13:1-7). He determined a division between the two camps should take place (Gen. 13:7-8). The man of God offered his nephew, Lot, the choice between the plains of Jordan and Canaan. Lot, thinking he outmaneuvered his uncle Abraham, chose the well watered plains of Jordan sensing it would bless him exceedingly. Lot's choice brought serious consequences on himself and his family. Verse 11 shows Lot choosing the plain of Jordan and in the next verse (12) he "pitched his tent toward Sodom." The chain of events led to the loss of his entire family save his two daughters (Gen. 19:30). The cause and effect revolving the choices of Abraham and Lot is striking. These men made decisions that led in two different directions; the same happens to us today if we fail to exercise good judgment (Matt. 7:13-14).

Judas Iscariot is an example of a man who brought problems on himself. On the positive scale the disciple possessed talents worthy of recognition. Jesus consequently chose Judas to serve as an apostle, and to receive the powers of that office (Matt. 10:1-4). However, no one but Judas was responsible for his death (27:3-5). The earliest recorded hint by Christ concerning Judas occurred about one year before the crucifixion. Jesus said, "But there are some of you that believed not. For Jesus knew from the beginning who they were that believed not, and who should betray him" (John 6:64). Jesus further underscores the evil in Judas, "Have not I chosen you twelve, and one of you is a devil?" (John 6:70). Jesus did not say that Judas was a demon, but a devil used only of Satan himself to whom Judas had surrendered. The events taking place in the life of Judas stemmed from his own heart punctuated by the decisions he made. The betrayer could not place blame on any one, but himself (Matt. 12:30).

RESPONSES TO THE LAW OF NATURE

The presence of the earth, its location, and position did not happen per chance. Genesis chapter one indicates perfect design and order by an Infinite Architect, God (Gen. 1:1). Surveying the skies on a clear night and reflecting upon the existence, power, and wisdom of the Creator gives us an understanding of the laws of nature stamped on our planet. David said, "The heavens declare the glory of God; and the firmament sheweth his handywork" (Psm. 19:1). The "heavens" or material heavens that appear to the eyes announce and proclaim God's glory. Paul acknowledges, "For the invisible things of him since the creation of the world are clearly seen, being perceived through the things that are made, even his everlasting power and divinity; that they may be without excuse" (Rom. 1:20).

God has created our earth so that nature follows

certain patterns. Weather patterns with precision instruments allow meteorologists to map out their forecast of weather conditions around the world. The earth is constructed with oceans and land areas, mountains and valleys. Some sections on earth receive a great deal of rain while other places, like deserts, receive little rainfall. There are rainy seasons, tornado seasons and dry seasons. If a person lives in a dry section of the world, he cannot accuse God of having a personal dislike for him because his area does not receive rain.

In his defense of God in Lystra, Paul stated, "He did good, and gave us rain from heaven, and fruitful seasons, filling our hearts with food and gladness" (Acts 14:17). God has arranged for the seasons found in nature. Those who live in tornado lanes or hurricane territory can expect tornadoes or hurricanes. God cannot be blamed for individual tragedies brought about by nature. Rain and sun are available for good and evil people alike (Matt. 5:45).

The certainty and compassion of our Creator shows unceasing care for man with needful and refreshing showers of rain. The sun and stars move by fixed laws, whose operation we can see and anticipate. The falling of rain is regulated by laws which we cannot describe, and it seems directly from the hollow of God's hand. David in this setting said, "Who covereth the heaven with clouds; who prepareth rain for the earth" (Psm. 147:8). Let us remember that God has instituted specific laws in nature and all should respect them with reverent awe.

SURROUNDING CIRCUMSTANCES

We see daily on local and national news outlets about young women abducted and atrociously murdered. Children on a daily basis are kidnapped, sexually molested and brutally killed. These are senseless acts that provoke us to moral outrage. Consider the twin towers falling down (9-11-01) with almost 3,000 Americans dying from the act of brain washed terrorists. These events and countless others do not seem just, and seeing the judicial system fall short in their responsibility compounds the frustration. Let us come to terms with the fact that all the books will not be balanced in this world, which accurately represent the horrors and crimes taking place in society. Solomon pointed out, "There is a vanity which is done upon the earth; that there be just men, unto whom it happeneth according to the work of the wicked; again, there be wicked men, to whom it happeneth according to the work of the righteous: I said that this also is vanity" (Eccl. 8:14).

Both good and evil people have their successes and failures. We hear of those speaking of the wicked that seem to prosper more than the righteous. David discussed this in Psalm 73 in some depth. Instead of righteousness and wickedness, circumstances might be the reason something good or bad takes place.

TIME AND CHANCE

Being at the right place at the right time or being present when an opportunity arises can determine what happens to us. Solomon wrote, "The race is not to the swift, nor the battle to the strong, nor bread to the wise, nor riches to men of understanding, nor favor to men of skill; But time and chance happen to them all" (Eccl. 9:11).

Henry Ford (automobile), Thomas Edison (light bulb), Alexander Graham Bell (telephone), and Benjamin Franklin (electricity) were men at the right place and time to accomplish amazing feats. This list of inventors did not succeed without sacrifice and dedication. Many of them experienced failure and disappointment, but with perseverance and resolve with timing and chance they succeeded.

Abraham Lincoln happened to live at the right time in history to become one of the great leaders of our nation. Had the man from Illinois been born at another time he might have been an unknown backwoods lawyer. In the age of television with thirty second television spots Lincoln likely would not have been elected as president of the United States.

The children of Israel "did that which was evil in the sight of the Lord: and the Lord delivered them into the hands of Midian for seven years"(Judg. 6:1). God's people, Israel, greatly destitute and suffering with hunger cried out to the Lord for help (Judg. 6:7). Gideon, selected by the Lord, became leader of Israel against the oppressive Midianites (Judg. 6:14). Gideon offered excuses stating, "My family is poor in Manasseh, and I am the least in my father's house" (Judg. 6:15). Gideon painted himself unqualified due to his family background. Moses in like manner stated, "I am slow of speech, and of a slow tongue," (Exod. 4:10). Gideon, the judge of Israel, led his people with three hundred faithful soldiers against their enemy

(Judg. 7:21-22). Perhaps this faithful man of God did not consider himself ready to serve, but God knew as time and chance ushered him to a place of service.

THE DEVIL

Deciding where blame should go for our trials in life will not always come with certainty. Satan is a real being who opposes all good. Because of Satan's deceptive activities, God is blamed for many of the evil things Satan does. He and his allies can hinder servants of God seeking to do the Father's will.

Paul wrote concerning his desire to see the Thessalonian Christians, "Therefore we wanted to come to you - even I, Paul, time and again - but Satan hindered us" (1 Thess. 2:18). The devil works hard to keep the world under his control using all evil forces at his disposal (1 John 5:19). Those submissive to him will be "taken captive to do his will" (2 Tim. 2:26).

We can know why some things happen, but we may never know why everything happens. With certainty we know that God gives us good gifts (James 1:17). The devil uses his tools of destruction to harm and eliminate our relationship with God (1 Peter 5:8). The devil has worked through such people as the Sabeans who took Job's beasts of burden and killed his servants (Job 1:14-15). He used a great wind to destroy a house and kill Job's children (v. 19). False teachers are used as his messengers (2 Cor. 11:13-14).

God used the sea bringing turbulence with a great wind that motivated the sailors to throw Jonah overboard (Jonah 1:4). He worked through Satan to accomplish His purposes when he gave Paul a thorn in the flesh humbling the apostle (2 Cor. 12:7). He also works through people (Phil. 2:13).

The Father in heaven has all sources available to accomplish His purposes. However, one should not become so preoccupied with the events affecting our lives that we force blame on God. Neither does it mean that God forces people against their will.

THE GODHEAD INVOLVED

God is active in His world, but does not exert direct influence bringing instant happiness, nor does He turn all evil things that happen to the righteous. A striking episode of evil taking place occurs in the life of David. In the course of time David's sin precipitated bad choices, and evil followed him as well as the nation of Israel (2 Sam. 12:10-12; 24:12-17).

Applying Romans 8:28 to teach the Godhead causes everything that happens may overstate God's activities. In the setting of this verse, Paul is teaching that God works in various ways for the good of those who love Him. "And we know that all things work together for good, (even) to them who are the called according to (his) purpose" (Rom. 8:28). We object to the view stating *all* the afflictions, catastrophes, illness, and death of family and friends are good.

The night our family received friends at the funeral home for our deceased daughter we heard those say, "This was God's will that your daughter slipped away to eternity." Some were well-meaning people thinking they gave us comfort. Ironically, Christians repeated similar statements, "God has a plan and surely God took Bethany for an important purpose." Beloved, why disasters happen may include many reasons. We may not know the entire basis for this horrible event, but the Bible will give concrete answers to this difficult challenge in life.

We learn in Romans 8 that God has provided freedom from condemnation through Jesus' death (Rom. 8:2), righteousness (v. 4), a glorious resurrection (v. 11), an inheritance (vs. 16-17), hope of salvation (v. 24), and help of the Holy Spirit in prayer (vs. 26-27). God works in these ways for the benefit of those who love Him.

In Romans 8:28 the word, "*all*," Greek panta (accusative, masculine, singular), usually does not include every possible thing. Luke uses the same word by stating, "They wondered everyone at *all* things which Jesus did" (Luke 9:43). Luke writes *all* (pantov) that Jesus did and taught until the day He was taken up. Conversely, John said, "the world itself could not contain the books that would be written" concerning what Jesus did (John 21:25). This is but one of many examples of the limited use of the word "all" (see other examples in John 14:26; Phil. 4:13).

CONCLUSION

Our problems in life will come from a number of factors. God should not be blamed for all the evil that happens to us, and keep in mind the Creator may become compelled to exercise discipline on His children (Heb. 12:5-12). On the other hand, the devil might be the mitigating factor instead of God. We cannot always know the source of evil happening in our lives, therefore let us exercise caution in affixing blame.

The early Christians suffered trying circumstances and even Paul faced many hardships as a servant of Christ (2 Cor. 11:23-27). Nature and other people were the cause of many setbacks thwarting the efforts of this mission minded apostle. We must place our faith in God that whatever happens to us, as long as we are faithful servants, God is for us (Rom. 8:31).

Regardless of what happens in our lives, we must remain faithful to God. Job is our example of perseverance in the face of great disaster (James 5:11). He may not have known why he had to suffer. He only knew he must remain true to God regardless of what happened to him.

In all his adversity Job said, "Though He slay me, yet will I trust Him" (Job 13:15). This is the attitude we should have. Instead of worrying about what caused our troubles and trials of life, we must resolve to remain faithful to God whatever might happen (Rev. 2:10).

THOUGHT QUESTIONS

1. Why is it important to give answers to the question of human suffering?

2. Lot's decision to move to the plains of Jordan caused what kind of problem?

3. Why does the law of nature give insights to the tragedy that many face?

4. What Scriptures prove the devil is responsible for the suffering and disasters?

5. When our daughter died of an automobile accident, some said it was God's will. Is this statement true? How does that fit the teaching of Romans 8:28?

Our Health, A Blessing From God

16

How many times have we heard those say, "If one has good health he is rich beyond compare." The blessings from God and its value cannot fully become known until lost?" This often made statement comes with Biblical support, however it is difficult to grasp until stricken with a bedfast condition and depending on others for help. Many that read this article know of the author's illness and the bedfast state endured over the last nine plus years. Before my surgery in April of 1995 and later crippling condition caused by multiple sclerosis has given a clearer focus than any previous time.

God made man out of the dust of the ground, and with a single breath man became a living soul (Gen. 1:26-27, 2:7). The supreme creation of God, man, became a person made in His own image. No one can state with any degree of logic that the Creator's handiwork manifested itself through long periods that scientists call evolution. David said, "Know ye that the Lord he is God: it is he that made us, and not we ourselves; we are his people, and the sheep of his pasture" (Psm. 100:3; 95:6-7). These are the two grounds for our recognizing the Lord as God; first that "He hath made us;" secondly, that "we are His people and His sheep" – namely, by His having redeemed us (Acts 20:28).

Man finds his greatest purpose and most satisfying joy when giving himself to the Lord in humble service. Remembering the Creator in our youth is essential to happiness; the outgrowth of this commitment leads us to "Fear God and keep his commandments" (Eccl. 12:1, 12-13). Our bodies come forth as the instrument God has given to see with our eyes, hear the cries with our ears, moved with compassion by a willing heart and serving the deprived with our hands. Imagine how futile it would be without our bodies to love, compassion to show concern and generosity to minister as we see those reaching for help. Count yourself rich and fortunate if blessed with good health.

GOOD HEALTH MAKES US RICH
WHEN OUR BODIES GLORIFY GOD

The apostle Paul declares that the body is the temple of God (1 Cor. 6:19-20). During the Mosaic Age God's presence became universally recognized in the tabernacle, and later in the temple constructed by Solomon. Today the inspired apostle Paul points out the fundamental thesis of the Holy Spirit dwelling in our bodies (1 Cor. 6:19). What an astonishing statement made by the inspired writer! The declaration of the Holy Spirit dwelling in the child of God cannot be refuted. However, we must state the indwelling does not come through a miraculous fashion, but through the Word. Our bodies are holy and they should be used in the service of God alone. The temple of Solomon and all utensils were holy and separated from common and profane uses. Further, our bodies in like manner respect, praise and exalt the name of our holy God in heaven (Psm. 139:14, 44:8). Jesus once prayed that man "with one mind and one mouth glorify God, even the Father of our Lord Jesus Christ" (Rom. 15:6). Our bodies and health must become dedicated to the purpose of glorifying God. It is through our bodies that we glorify and pay homage to our Creator by serving Him in "reverence and godly fear (awe)" (Heb. 12:28). Jesus shows this truth, "I have glorified thee on the earth..." (John 17:4). Our service to God and the bodies that house our souls are holy, and all their members should dedicate themselves in the service of God alone. We belong to God and to Him are we accountable (2 Cor. 5:10; Heb. 9:27).

GOOD HEALTH MAKES US RICH
IF WE RESIST SATAN

Health is a blessing from God and neglecting our bodies through selfish means is sin (Rom. 8:13; 2 Peter 2:14). Paul writes that our body "is not our own." Since our body belongs to God we should follow the directives of doctors and the normal care and maintenance expected. We owe our bodies respect by refusing to ignore it through harm or neglect. The conscientious Christian understands with greater clarity about bodily care. We do this by having regular checkups, exercise, proper diet and whatever it takes to see God's temple respected. Recently the AMA has released information that one-third of all Americans are obese or overweight. Is this something that Christians can ignore? Do we not have the responsibility and mandate from God and His Word to prevent such from occurring? This is becoming a widespread problem in our culture and the child of God should use self-control to prevent this from happening (Gal. 5:25).

If our body is the temple of the Holy Spirit and we overindulge with drugs, tobacco, alcohol or by overeating we have ignored God's precious gift entrusted to us. Our bodies have become God's instrument to accomplish His bidding; therefore we have no right to misuse it at our pleasure. As stewards we must have the knowledge of this responsibility and with all vigilance take care of our bodies remembering its primary use is to carry out His will. James 3:6 affirms the misuse of the tongue will defile the whole body. Everything we do in the body will either destroy or glorify our bodies before God. Sins of fornication, thievery, speaking lies, drunkenness, and sowing discord are a misuse of the body. Conversely acts of kindness, love, encouraging the weak, teaching the gospel to a friend will exalt the Father in heaven. Our God has given us a body, albeit temporary, as a vehicle to perform positive works while we live on this earth.

Caution, let us beware of Satan using his many devices to crush us in the mission our Father in heaven has prearranged (Matt. 28:18-20; Eph. 4:11-12; 1 Peter 5:8).

How many times have we seen those ignore their bodies allowing themselves to become susceptible to disease and illness cutting short the span of years to serve God? Beloved, let us practice the Biblical principle of "temperance" or "self—control" and reject all practices and appetites that will contribute or threaten our health. Let us be aware of the inspired words, "Resist the devil and he will flee from you. Draw nigh to God, and he will draw nigh to you" (James 4:7-8).

GOOD HEALTH EXPRESSES
THE KINDNESS OF OUR GOD

We know that our bodies are a temporary vessel and like any other it will deteriorate with time. We must remember the importance of our bodies and dedicate it to God. The body dedicated and set apart for Him must remain clean and pure for His service. Paul addresses the Thessalonian Christians for living unclean lives stating, "That every one of you should know how to possess his vessel (body) in sanctification and honor" (1 Thess. 4:4). Using our bodies for the purpose of self-gratification and sin rejects the basis for which we were created.

Before the universal flood (Gen. 6-9) man would typically live 900 years plus, but in the post flood era the life span changed dramatically with those living only about fourscore years. The Psalmist declared,

"The days of our years are threescore and ten, and if by reason of strength they be fourscore (80 years)" (Psm. 90:10). This gift is a blessing which we cannot calculate with the most sophisticated equipment. If blessed with such a gift it would hasten us to pray thanking the Creator for the blessing received. As we look around to see our fellowman and Christians alike suffer with various ills and physical maladies we should count our blessings for the gift of good health (James 1:17).

Recognizing this great blessing makes us rich beyond compare and should motivate us to thank God for such a gift. However, we must know that in due season such will not always be the case. Becoming ill or stricken with a disease, heart trouble, cancer or other maladies will humble us like all others that have lived before us. Illness and bad health is a test to our faith and how we respond will distinguish between those giving loyalty to God or Satan.

The renowned patriarch, Job, passed the test of physical affliction with determination and perseverance. This faithful man of God while enduring painful sores from head to foot rejected the foolish challenge of his wife to "curse God and die" (Job 2:9). Job in effect said shall we receive the good and not the bad. Anyone that reads this chapter knows in the course of time misfortune and adversity will take place in our earthly pilgrimage (Heb. 11:13). Life is not always a bouquet of roses. Thorns will appear occasionally. Job understood this principle and he serves as a model for all to imitate. This man of patience understood that it would be the height of foolishness to question God. Remember, the source of every good and perfect gift comes from God (James 1:17).

The good health we enjoy is a blessing, but ill health brings challenges defying human description. James says, "Count it all joy when you fall into diver's temptations (trials) knowing that to prove your faith worketh patience" (James 1:2-3). We are not to consider temptations (trials) as a punishment, a curse, or a calamity, but as a fit subject of approval. We have all faced a variety of tasks that required resolute determination, physical aptitude, and mental fitness. Taking a math quiz of unusual difficulty or competing on the athletic field and excelling gives one a sense of joy and satisfaction. These two endeavors were difficult and challenging, however, succeeding brought gladness beyond compare. Enduring criticism and ridicule in the face of those opposing Truth and righteousness challenges every child of God. Jesus put it this way, "Blessed are ye, when men shall revile you, and persecute you, and shall say all manner of evil against you falsely, for my sake. Rejoice, and be exceeding glad: for great is your reward in heaven..." (Matt. 5:11-12).

This disabled preacher, bedridden for nearly nine years, has gained a better perspective of health's blessings. Seeing these events has caused me to realize how often we forget the daily blessings of waking-up, showering, getting dressed, going to work, and providing for our family as a normal life style. Exchanging love for our families while using every opportunity to serve our fellowman in service to God is the purpose of our existence. Life is uncertain and whatever comes we must adjust with faith and courage. Let us all consider, *"Health, A Blessing From God."*

GOOD HEALTH BRINGS US TO FAITHFUL SERVICE

Good health, as stated, comes from God as a blessing exceeding silver and gold. Possessing good health gives us opportunities to fulfill duties of life that those with serious illness cannot visualize. Memories of those special times come with amazing clarity giving that period exceptional meaning. This period of my life seems distant, but likewise it appears as though it were yesterday.

The writer of the Revelation through John wrote the Ephesian church saying, "be thou faithful unto death, and I will give thee a crown of life" (Rev. 2:10). A commentator, Adam Clarke, thinks that Polycarp may have received this letter. According to historians Polycarp, an aged elder in the church, suffered much and finally consumed with fire in martyrdom. The Church at Ephesus endured much at this time described as the "synagogue of Satan" (Rev. 2:9). Persecution would be great, but in the final analysis they must be firm to the end if faced with extreme suffering or death by natural means. Faithful service to God includes those with good health and likewise those that do not.

Jesus depicted as the Son of man in Matthew 25: 31-46, gathered all nations and separated them as the shepherd divided his sheep from the goats. This wonderful text describes the shepherd judging those not for what they did, but what they did not do. He gives a list of items that should give us pause and serious reflection: feeding the hungry, water for those athirst, entertaining strangers, clothing the naked, caring for the sick, and visiting the imprisoned. Those on the right hand were given entrance to the kingdom as they faithfully served those in need (v. 34, 40). In contrast those on the left hand did not possess a compassionate heart failing to serve those in want. Jesus said, "Depart from me, ye cursed, into the everlasting fire, prepared for the devil and his angels" (Matt. 25:41).

Good health allows us to serve those in need symbolizing the Master as he ministered to those poor and disadvantaged souls. We must all reach out to those suffering physically and spiritually. Paul writes, "As we have therefore opportunity, let us do good unto all men, especially unto them who are of the household of faith" (Gal. 6:10). Reader friend, consider that special shut-in that needs visiting, the person recovering from surgery, or those losing a loved one. We have plenty to do and how shameful to neglect those needing our attention.

Those of us confined to a hospital bed have occasions to serve others. Sue Ellen Frasier, deceased, but a dear sister in Christ when we knew her many years ago. Sister Frasier confined to her home and connected to an oxygen tank, due to severe breathing problems, faithfully served as a Christian. She never wanted to talk about her health, but expressed keen interest in others. Always interested in the local church she inquired about the sick, shut-ins, absentees, and others. She often said, "Who can I call to encourage that wayward Christian to return to their first love?" This Christian woman served as a role model, although confined, yet faithfully served in the only way she could. We read of woman in Mark 14:1-9 that created a stir by breaking an alabaster box of ointment and pouring it on the Lord's head. The disciples of Jesus led by Judas rebuked the woman, but the Lord said, "Let her alone, why trouble ye her? She hath wrought a good work on me." He further said, "She hath done what she could" (Mark 14:6, 8). Men and women have their roles to play, but Jesus would not let Mary's good work become a useless exercise (John 12:3).

THOUGHT QUESTIONS

1. Where does man find his greatest purpose in life?

2. What does the temple of Solomon and our bodies have in common?

3. How important is it to keep healthy bodies? Why is it wrong to abuse our bodies?

4. Job's wife challenged her husband to "curse God and die." How did he react to this test? How would you respond if the tables were turned?

5. The woman that showed love for Jesus was ridiculed. What did Jesus say? How would you respond if someone ridiculed you for doing good?